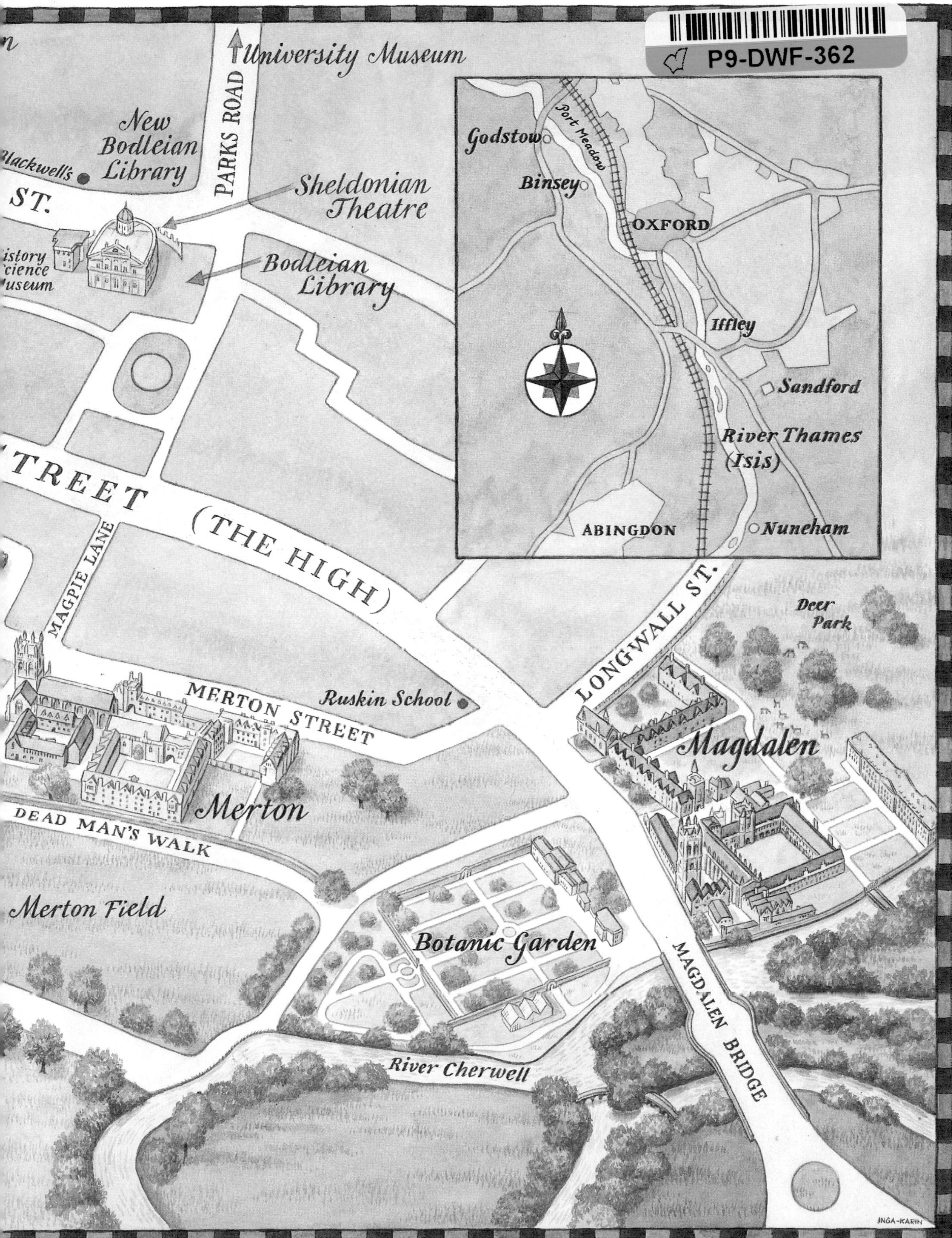
University Museum
PARKS ROAD
New Bodleian Library
Blackwell's
ST.
Sheldonian Theatre
Bodleian Library
Godstow
Port Meadow
Binsey
OXFORD
Iffley
Sandford
River Thames (Isis)
ABINGDON
Nuneham
STREET (THE HIGH)
MAGPIE LANE
LONGWALL ST.
Deer Park
MERTON STREET
Ruskin School
Magdalen
Merton
DEAD MAN'S WALK
Merton Field
Botanic Garden
MAGDALEN BRIDGE
River Cherwell
INGA-KARIN

Rabén & Sjögren Stockholm

Originally published in Sweden by Rabén & Sjögren
under the title *Sagan om Alice i Verkligheten*

Layout by Christina Björk and Inga-Karin Eriksson
Printed in Italy
Library of Congress catalog card number: 93-662
First edition, 1993

ISBN 91-29-62242-5

The other ALICE

The Story of Alice Liddell and Alice in Wonderland

CHRISTINA BJÖRK
PICTURES BY INGA-KARIN ERIKSSON

Translated by Joan Sandin

R&S
BOOKS

Stockholm New York London Adelaide Toronto

We think we have caught
Lewis Carroll;
we look again and see an Oxford clergyman.
We think we have caught
the Reverend C.L. Dodgson
— we look again and see a fairy elf.
Virginia Woolf

Contents

Christina's awful little Christ Church photo from 1955

Inga-Karin rowing in Alice's wake

Lewis Carroll Society's conference cake, 1989

The Tom Tower staircase

Foreword

● One day, when I was about ten years old, I was home from school with a cold. When my father came home that night, he brought me a book. It was called *Alice's Adventures in Wonderland.* I had never read anything like it. It was so remarkable I had to stay home all the next day to finish reading it.

When Alice fell down the rabbit hole, she landed in a totally different world. Since I was fascinated by other worlds, *Alice* became one of my favorite books. It was the unexpected, and also the unexplainable, that made the book so exciting.

When I was seventeen, I took a trip to England with my father. We were in Oxford, but all I remember about the city is that we visited Christ Church, and I learned that Lewis Carroll had lived there. The other day I came across this awful little picture I took with my father's old box camera (August 1955).

I don't remember if any of my childhood friends read *Alice,* but now, after all these years, I hear that some of them did, and *didn't* like it. They thought it was too strange; some were even frightened by it. One girl burned the book so she wouldn't have to see it. What different reactions people can have!

As an adult, I have come across a number of books about Lewis Carroll, the author, and when I found out that Alice had been a real person, I became more and more interested in his story. I wish that I could have met Lewis Carroll (or Charles Dodgson, which was his real name). What an imagination he had!

I heard that there was a society for Carroll enthusiasts, the Lewis Carroll Society. I joined immediately. In 1989, I attended the society's first international conference in Oxford. There I stayed at Christ Church and met friends of *Alice* from all over the world.

It was then I decided to do a book about Alice and Mr. Dodgson, although there already were tons of books about them. Even so, there wasn't one that was fun for kids to read, too.

I brought Inga-Karin Eriksson (the illustrator of this book) into the project, and we took off for Oxford together. We stayed at Christ Church, where the whole story began more than a hundred years ago. There, and in the area surrounding Oxford, we followed in the footsteps of Alice and Mr. Dodgson, hiking, rowing, and picnicking. We searched in libraries and secondhand bookstores; we snooped around in archives, interviewed Carroll experts, took pictures, sketched. It was one of many visits to Oxford.

Even though everything happened such a long time ago, we do know quite a lot about Mr. Dodgson's life. Many of his diaries and letters have been saved. A number of the children he befriended, including Alice, have later told and written about their childhood friendships with him; he remained one of their best childhood memories.

With all of this, we put together OUR story. We can't know EXACTLY what everything was like, or just how it happened, since we weren't there. That's why our story is a "mischmasch" of what we KNOW happened, what PROBABLY happened, and what COULD have happened.

Bob the Bat, for example, really existed. He was named Bob and lived in an upper left desk drawer, even though it was another girl who told about him (but Alice probably knew, too). We know that Alice saw the dodo at the museum, but we do not know exactly how it was displayed and we have only imagined that she might have dreamed about it afterward. If you want to know the exact details, you can try to find some of the books listed on page 92.

We never intended for this book to be

a scholarly work (there are so many of those already); what we wanted to do was make it more fun for you when you read *Alice.* You'll be able to recognize some of the things in the story, just as the real Alice did when she heard it for the first time.

Maybe this book can show you how to do some of the tricks and riddles and games that Mr. Dodgson taught Alice. We thought they could be just as much fun today as they were more than a hundred years ago.

Maybe the book can also give a glimpse of what it was like to be a child in the Victorian era (named after Queen Victoria, who reigned over Britain for many years).

P.S. If you are planning a trip to Oxford, you can easily locate the different places in the story on the maps at the beginning and the end of this book. (There are some tips as well on pages 90–91.) A lot of things are still much the same there. It's true that the monkeys are gone from the Botanic Garden, but the ginkgo tree is still alive, even if Mr. Dodgson and all of his child-friends have been dead for a long time.

Thank you

There are many people who have helped us with this book:
Edward Wakeling of the Lewis Carroll Society is the person we've questioned the most. He's also been kind enough to check our facts, both text and pictures. He also taught us 42^3 and came up with two excellent snail names.
Anne Clark Amor, together with *Ellis Hillman* one of the founders of the Lewis Carroll Society, has also answered a lot of our questions. In addition, we found her two books about Carroll and Alice to be very useful.
Graham Ovenden generously shared old Carroll photographs with us.
The Governing Body of Christ Church also generously lent us old photographs.
Jennie Bradshaw, John Wing, and *Janet McMullin* of Christ Church Library found books, pictures, and other material for us in the archives.
Bishop Krister Stendahl we especially thank, for without him we would never have got into the holiest of all places: Alice's own nursery.
The Reverend E. W. Heaton, Dean of Christ Church, allowed us into his private quarters to snoop around and take pictures.
Ann Gordon, the Dean's secretary, arranged for us to visit a number of important places in Christ Church.
Les Jones and *Tony Everett* showed us Charles Dodgson's rooms and the bell tower, Tom Tower.
Sarah Levitt, of Gunnersbury Park Museum in London, showed us her collection of children's clothes from the 1860s and answered our many questions.
Wynne Bartlett showed us around the town of Guildford.
Jean Gattegno, Carroll expert in Paris, answered questions and recommended books.
Lena Törnqvist at the Swedish Institute for Children's Books helped us to find books. As did *Opie Collection,* Oxford.
Jan Lundberg built a period model of a rowboat for us.
Göran Österlund helped us take pictures in Oxford and patiently gave us good advice.
Jan Sundfeldt was also very patient and a good rower.
Joan Sandin translated all our words and Swedish puns into English and managed to glue them together from all the papers that coiled out of her fax in the middle of the night.
Roger Bowen, of the Himmel Park Volleyball Society, helped the translator give the conversations a more British flavor.
Elisabeth Dyssegaard, Carmen Gomezplata, and *Elaine Chubb,* checked the facts one more time and also the translation into English.
Maija Zeile-Westrup, Susanne Öhman-Sundén, and *Kate Meurling* of Rabén & Sjögren Publishers (Stockholm, Sweden) believed in the idea, encouraged us, and waited patiently for the book to be ready.
Ruth Dingley, Kate's ninety-six-year-old English grandmother, told us how she had loved the *Alice* books and that she had played Alice in a school production.
Mavis Batey, Lisbet Gabrielsson, Selwyn Goodacre, Gunnila Grimhall, and *Sara Overödder* all in different ways contributed to this book. As did *Marina Ehrling* and *Rose Hughes* at the British Tourist Authority of Stockholm and London.

Once upon a time . . .

lease, Mr. Dodgson," begged Alice, as soon as she had hopped into the boat. "Please, Mr. Dodgson, tell us a story."

"Shouldn't we row up to Godstow first, and save the story until our picnic?" said Mr. Dodgson, putting the oars in place.

"No!" cried all three girls. "Start the story *now*!"

"Only if it's not *too* exciting," said Mr. Duckworth (one of Mr. Dodgson's good friends, who manned the other pair of oars). "Otherwise, Alice will never be able to manage the rudder."

"Yes, I will," said Alice, as she tried holding it steady. (If you don't do that, the boat just goes around in circles, which is very embarrassing.)

"But if we start the story now," said Mr. Dodgson, "what will we have left for our picnic?"

"Tell a long story, then," said Lorina (the oldest).

"One that will last all the way home," said Edith (who was the youngest).

"There are no stories that long," said Mr. Duckworth.

"Oh yes, there are," said Alice. "How do you suppose they fill up entire books? But please, don't tell a story that's already in a book."

Mr. Dodgson rested on his oars a few minutes. He stared at the sky as if he might find a *really* long story hiding up there.

But actually it was just the opposite. His story came from down below; you might say he found it underground . . .

It was perfectly quiet that hot summer day on the river. There wasn't even the sound of an oar, or the chirp of a bird, or the buzz of a fly. The boat moved slowly forward.

"Once upon a time . . ." Mr. Dodgson began hesitantly.

"You always start like that," said Alice.

"All real stories start like that," said Mr. Dodgson. "Once upon a time . . . there was a little girl whose name was . . . Alice!"

Whoops! Alice steered a little crooked.

"It was just as warm and sunny as today," Mr. Dodgson continued. "Alice sat on the riverbank with her sister."

"Was that me?" Edith wondered.

"No, it was probably Ina," said Mr. Dodgson (he meant Lorina), because she was reading one of those terribly dull books with no pictures or conversations. Alice was bored, so bored that she almost fell asleep. But then suddenly . . ."

"What do you mean, suddenly?" All three girls leaned forward.

So Mr. Dodgson told them how a white rabbit (with pink eyes) came running by, saying, "Oh dear! Oh dear! I shall be too late!" And then when the rabbit pulled a watch out of its waistcoat pocket (a rabbit with a waistcoat pocket!) and dashed off, well, Alice was simply forced to follow it across the field and down into a large rabbit hole under the hedge. She crawled down a kind of long tunnel, and suddenly . . .

"Why are you steering like that?" said Mr. Dodgson.

"Oh, sorry," said Alice. "But what happened after 'suddenly'?"

"Well, the tunnel began dipping downward, more and more, until it simply became a deep hole that Alice was falling down."

Since Mr. Dodgson didn't really know what would happen next, he let Alice continue falling a long time before she reached the bottom. And there the most remarkable things happened. Sometimes Mr. Dodgson pretended to fall asleep so he would have time to make up the next part of the story.

"And that's all till next time," said Mr. Dodgson, halfway through the story.

"Ah," said Alice. "But it *is* next time."

And so he continued the story. When they had found a good place for a picnic, in the shade of a big haystack, Mr. Duckworth asked if Mr. Dodgson was making up his story on the spot.

"Yes, I'm inventing as we go along," replied Mr. Dodgson.

And it turned out the way Edith wanted it to. The story lasted all through the picnic and all the way home as well. At times, bits and pieces of old stories that the girls recognized slipped in. And some of the strange characters that popped up were familiar: the dodo, for example, the extinct bird they had seen in the museum.

Mr. Dodgson didn't get the girls home until after eight-thirty that evening. Everybody was tired, especially Mr. Dodgson, who was close to exhaustion after the long story.

"Thank you, Mr. Dodgson, for the wonderful story," said Ina.

"And for making it last all the way home," said Edith, who had nearly fallen asleep on the stairs.

"Please, Mr. Dodgson," begged Alice, "write down the story for me."

"Well, we don't usually write them down, you know," said Mr. Dodgson. "Or even write them up. I'll tell a new one next time."

"No," said Alice. "This one may *not* just disappear. After all, it was about me. Besides, it was *special.* Oh, please! Promise!"

Alice had to pester him over and over before Mr. Dodgson got started. But then he did it painstakingly. He printed the whole story by hand, and he even illustrated it. When it was finally finished, he gave it to Alice as a present.

In 1865, the book was professionally printed and published. The author's name was given as Lewis Carroll, but Lewis Carroll and Charles Dodgson were really the same person.

The first copy of the printed book was given to Alice, of course. But by then she had gotten so much older she was almost tired of stories.

It's a pity, Mr. Dodgson thought, that girls have to grow up. They're a lot more fun when they are small; they love stories and other good things. When they turn into elegant ladies, they become very boring.

But all of that happened many, many years ago. Neither Mr. Dodgson nor Alice is alive today. The story, however, lives on — the story that Charles Dodgson told Alice Liddell on July 4, 1862, a warm and sunny day, while boating on the river Thames (or Isis, as it is called in Oxford).

Every year the book comes out in a new edition somewhere in the world; every year new children get to hear Alice's own story, *Alice's Adventures In Wonderland,* for the first time. So it must be true that there's something special about the story, just as Alice said.

And there must have been something *special* about Mr. Dodgson, who could tell such a good story. That's what *this* book is about. It's also about Alice Liddell, who was Charles Dodgson's very best child-friend. Until she got too big, of course.

Once upon a time . . .

Bob the Bat's Adventure

Once upon a time there was a girl who had just turned seven years old. Her name was Alice Pleasance Liddell. She was called Alice after a princess and Pleasance after her grandfather's sister. Liddell was her last name.

Oh, what a long name, thought Alice, writing it under her picture in Mr. Dodgson's photo album, as he had asked her to do.

"Once upon a time . . ." said Mr. Dodgson, and Alice stopped writing.

"Once upon a time there was a bat by the name of Bob," Mr. Dodgson continued, "who lived in . . ."

". . . the upper left desk drawer!" said Alice, putting down the album halfway through "Pleasance."

Alice Pleas

"Exactly," said Mr. Dodgson. "And he could . . ."

"Fly!" said Alice. "Oh, please let him out!"

Mr. Dodgson took out Bob the Bat. He was made of wire and black gauze. Mr. Dodgson wound him up with a rubber band and let him go. Bob flew around Mr. Dodgson's room for nearly thirty seconds. Round and round, out of control, since there was no way to steer him. First he crashed into the lamp (but he missed the camera) . . . then into the fireplace, and out again (even blacker). Then . . . oh no! Bob flew right out the window!

CRASH! The sound of broken dishes or glass! Mr. Dodgson and Alice ran over to the window. Oh, what a mess!

"Bob has no manners," said Mr. Dodgson.

What had Bob done? Well, he had landed in the middle of a bowl of salad that a college servant was carrying across the garden. Now the young man, the bowl, the salad, and Bob were all one big jumble on the ground.

"Sorry!" Mr. Dodgson shouted down to the servant. "Bring the bat up here, and I'll make it up to you."

Alice had to sit down or she would have fallen over laughing.

"Oh yes, stay sitting just like that," said Mr. Dodgson. "I must take a picture of you . . ."

"Oh, not again," said Alice to herself.

"But it's too dark in here; we'll take it outside, instead. Quick as a flash."

Quick as a flash, thought Alice. No flash ever lasted that long.

In those days it wasn't as simple to take a picture as it is today. The camera was a new invention, a large, clumsy-looking box. Instead of a small roll of film, Mr. Dodgson used a square piece of glass that had been dipped in two different chemicals. The second one made the glass sensitive to light. It had to be put into the camera quickly (without exposing it to light), while it was still wet. The camera, tripod, Alice, and a chair all had to be set up outside. Mr. Dodgson took the lens cover off the camera, counted to 45, and then put it back on again. If Alice didn't sit perfectly still the whole time, she would be blurry in the picture.

Now, when Alice saw the broken salad bowl down in the garden, she started laughing all over again. How would she ever manage to sit still?

"Think of something sad," said Mr. Dodgson.

"What!" said Alice. "For a full forty-five seconds?"

"What about forty-two, then?" said Mr. Dodgson, starting to count. Alice sat perfectly still.

"Forty-two!" shouted Mr. Dodgson, putting the lens cover back in place. "How ever did you do it?"

"I thought of Willikens," said Alice.

Willikens was Alice's brother's kitten which had died after eating rat poison.

"But that was too sad," said Alice, "so I had to think of Bob the Bat for a bit. But that got to be too funny, so I had to switch to Willikens again. Back and forth like that the whole time."

"That was quite clever of you," said Mr. Dodgson. "Now, would you like to go up to the darkroom with me?"

Of course she would! Mr. Dodgson put the glass plate in the developing tank, full of a liquid that smelled both disgusting and exciting at the same time. After Mr. Dodgson had jiggled the tank for a while, Alice saw herself slowly begin to appear on the plate. Except it was an Alice with black skin and white hair. The image was reversed: everything that was really dark had become light; everything light was dark. It was a *negative.* Was it blurry or sharp?

"It's sharp," said Alice. "Hurrah!"

While Mr. Dodgson finished developing the negative, Alice went down to play with his music boxes. There were ten or twenty (maybe forty-two) of them; Alice hadn't really counted. Some were small ones made of ebony that you wound up with a key. When you opened the lid, they would begin to play. You could look into some of the boxes and watch the gears turn. If a music box broke, Mr. Dodgson would take out his tiniest screwdriver and fix it.

Imagine, Mr. Dodgson had almost as many toys as Alice did! The mechanical rabbit that popped up from inside a cabbage was the one she most wished were hers. And there were games, and lots of children's books . . .

"Why are you so playful?" asked Alice, when Mr. Dodgson came downstairs. "After all, you are a grownup, you know."

"I got quite a lot of practice when I was a child," said Mr. Dodgson.

Alice thought about that a minute.

And then Mr. Dodgson said, "Now we'll have some tea."

Mr. Dodgson boiled the water and poured it over the tea leaves. Then he walked back and forth, carrying the pot.

"Why are you doing that?" asked Alice.

"Well, you see, tea draws better when it can move around a bit," said Mr. Dodgson. "Once upon a time there was a T that only stood still. It became so depressed it had an attack of nerves and went all to pieces. Like this":

Mr. Dodgson drew a picture of how terrible it had been for poor T. And by that time the tea was ready. Alice ate quite a few scones with jam (jam that Mr. Dodgson's sister Fanny had made).

"Is Fanny as clever as you at playing?" Alice asked.

"Absolutely," said Mr. Dodgson. "I taught her how."

Naturally, Alice said, "What did you play?"

"This and that," answered Mr. Dodgson. "And sometimes everything possible. Even backwards. Speaking of which, I have invented backwards music. Would you like to hear it?"

Alice with one of Mr. Dodgson's music boxes

Mr. Dodgson took down his largest music box, his "American orguinette." When he cranked a long strip of punched paper through it, it played a tune. It sounded like a small organ.

"Now I'll put the strips in upside down and backwards," said Mr. Dodgson. "Then the melody will be played backwards."

Backwards music sounded very strange.

"It's a pity I haven't figured out how to make time go backwards as well," said Mr. Dodgson.

"Would that be a good idea?" Alice wondered.

"Yes," said Mr. Dodgson. "Then you wouldn't grow up and get bigger all the time."

"But I want to get bigger," said Alice. "A *little* bigger."

"I think you're just right the way you are," said Mr. Dodgson. "Perhaps later you may become an elegant lady, and then you'll forget how to play."

"Not I," said Alice.

Mr. Dodgson Makes a Handkerchief Rabbit

That evening Mr. Dodgson printed the negative. The print was the reverse of the negative, so this time Alice's hair and skin were the right color. That kind of picture is called a *positive.*

The next day Mr. Dodgson brought the picture over to the Liddells'. Both he and Alice lived at Christ Church, a college at Oxford University in England. Mr. Dodgson lived there because he taught mathematics and logic at the college, and Alice because her father was dean. Dean Liddell was the head of the college as well as being in charge of Oxford Cathedral, which was situated in the college.

To visit the Liddells, Mr. Dodgson simply walked across the college quad and came to a brown door that said DEANERY on it. That's where Alice lived.

A servant named Francis answered the door and went to get Mrs. Liddell, an elegant and rather prim lady. But when Mr. Dodgson showed her the photograph of Alice she was delighted.

"Do come in, Mr. Dodgson," she said. "What a lovely profile she has. But next time I should like you to take a picture of all three girls, not just Alice."

Mr. Dodgson promised. He asked if he could show Alice the picture.

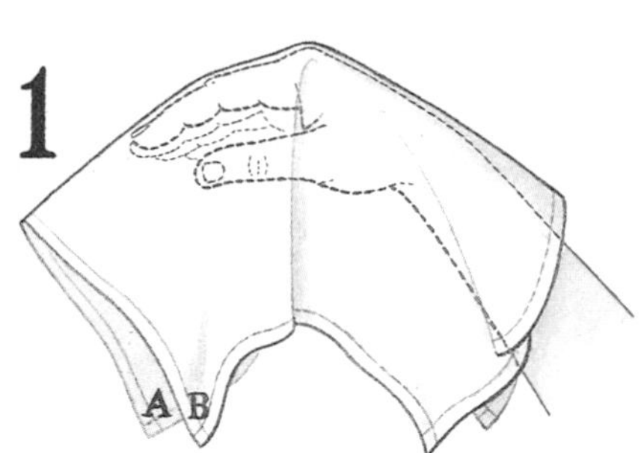

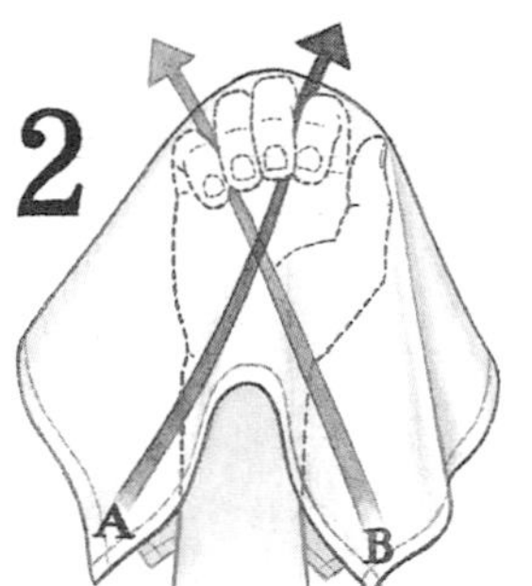

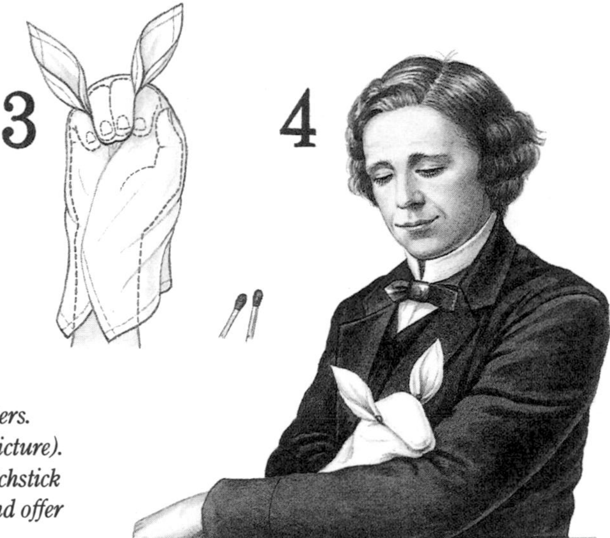

1. *Put a handkerchief over your right hand.*
2. *Cross the front corners (A and B) and pull them up between your fingers.*
3. *Now the rabbit has ears. Tuck them tightly between your fingers (see picture).*
4. *Stuff the edge of the handkerchief into your right sleeve, and push matchstick ends under the "ears" for eyes. Move your middle and ring fingers, and offer your rabbit a cookie!*

"Of course," said Alice's mother. "Francis, show Mr. Dodgson to the nursery."

"Oh, Mr. Dodgson!" shouted Alice. "The photograph!"

Alice's big sister, Lorina, and little sister, Edith, admired the picture. Miss Prickett, the girls' governess, wanted to see it, too.

"Your mother has asked me to take a picture of all three of you," said Mr. Dodgson.

"Then we must wear our new print dresses," said Ina.

"Mr. Dodgson, would you like tea?" asked Alice.

Just then Phoebe, the girls' nurse, arrived with their dinner. They always ate in the nursery, never with their parents in the dining room. It was good that Mr. Dodgson felt more at home in the nursery than in the dining room.

"Imagine having a rabbit like that one in the cabbage; I should like that!" said Alice.

"Alice!" corrected her big sister, Ina. "That's not polite."

"Sorry," said Alice. "I didn't mean just that particular rabbit, but we really could use a rabbit."

"That can be arranged in no time," said Mr. Dodgson.

He took out his pocket handkerchief and folded and twisted it until it looked just like a little rabbit.

"Now it's my turn," said Ina, unfolding the handkerchief and putting it over her own hand.

And then it was Alice's turn. Her rabbit looked more like a rat. Edith's looked like . . . well, it's hard to say what Edith's looked like.

"But now there's no time to take pictures before it gets dark. I shall ask your mother if we may do it tomorrow, instead."

Yes, it was always safest to check with Mrs. Liddell. Once Mr. Dodgson had asked Miss Prickett for permission. Mrs. Liddell had been so angry that she took all the children and left when Mr. Dodgson arrived. You couldn't be too careful with Mrs. Liddell.

Edith, Ina, and Alice

One Man Who Was Really Two

Mr. Dodgson's full name was Charles Lutwidge Dodgson. Charles was his father's name, Lutwidge was his mother's maiden name, and Dodgson his family name. When Alice was seven years old, Mr. Dodgson was twenty-seven. Alice thought that was old.

Charles Dodgson dressed mostly in black: he wore a long jacket that looked old-fashioned, even for that time. He usually wore a top hat, and he *always* wore gloves, no matter how warm it was. But he *never* wore an overcoat, no matter how cold it was! Mr. Dodgson walked with his back so straight that people said he looked as if he "had swallowed an iron poker."

Even as a boy, he had been unusually good in arithmetic. His father had taught him. His best marks in school were in mathematics, and it was taken for granted that he would continue his math studies at the university.

He taught mathematics and even wrote mathematics textbooks.

Mr. Dodgson, as the children called him (they never called him by his first name!), had one problem. He was shy. Maybe it was because he had a stutter; the more he thought about it, the worse it became.

He thought the hardest thing was to teach lazy students at Christ Church. And some considered him to be the world's dullest teacher.

Self-portrait in front of his mathematics students

Still, Mr. Dodgson liked living at Christ Church. In order to stay there, he had to remain single. It would have been even better to have become an ordained minister. But he did not become one. Was that because of his stutter? (He became a deacon instead.)

Generally, he *didn't* stutter when he was with children. He wasn't a bit shy then, and his stutter almost disappeared.

When he called on friends, he was happy to visit the nursery. Parents would find him under a table pretending to be a bear, or sitting with all the children on his lap, telling a story.

His Uncle Skeffington inspired Mr. Dodgson to take up photography, something few people practiced at that time. It was a good way to get acquainted with children, he discovered.

"Oh, what beautiful children!" he would say to a mother in a park. "I should like to make a likeness of them."

And then he would be invited to visit.

That was how he got acquainted with the Liddell children. He had asked permission to take a picture of the cathedral tower from their garden. But after his successful picture of Alice's big brother, Harry, he was frequently a welcome guest.

The Liddell children were his favorite child-friends. Alice was the one he liked best of all.

"Let's pretend . . ." was Alice's favorite expression. Mr. Dodgson's as well. Alice once really frightened her nice nanny, Phoebe, by shouting, "Let's

Self-portrait of Charles Dodgson (Lewis Carroll). In his diary (June 2, 1857) he wrote: "To try the lens, I took a picture of myself, for which Ina took off the cap, and of course considered it all her doing!" Was it this photo?

pretend you are a pork bone and I'm a hungry *hyena*!!!" Sometimes Alice pretended to be two people: "Now, listen here, Alice," she would say to herself. "I promise you there is no lion under the bed." "That's what you think!" the other Alice would reply.

You could say that Mr. Dodgson was also two people: the serious mathematics teacher and the playful grownup. Maybe he would have liked it better never to have grown up, but of course that would have been impossible. He had to do it, just like the rest of us.

Lions, Cats, Horses, and Alice's Father

Everything in this story, as you know, happened a very long time ago in Oxford, England. The first time Mr. Dodgson met Alice, she was almost four years old. We know it was April 26, 1856, because Mr. Dodgson wrote about it in his diary.

"I mark this day with a white stone," he added later.

That was something he wrote on especially happy days.

lice's father, Henry Liddell, was a well-educated man. He and a good friend, Robert Scott, had written a lexicon where you could look up the meanings of classical Greek words. The book was a success and was reprinted many times. Each time Alice's father added new words that he had discovered. And he received some money for each lexicon that was sold. (His lexicon is still used in schools today.)

With the money he earned, Dean Liddell built a handsome staircase, the Lexicon Staircase, up to the second floor, where the nursery was. On each newel post was a carved wooden lion.

In the evening, after Alice had said good night to her parents, she would *run* as fast as she could up the stairs, past all those lions. You never knew if one fine day (no, one fine night!) one of the lions might jump down from its post. Just to be on the safe side, Alice always checked under her bed before she went to sleep.

Harry 12 years

Lorina (Ina) 10 years

Arthur †

Alice 7 years

Dinah

Edith 5 years

Rhoda

Alice's father had also arranged to have a bathroom installed, with a real bathtub and a faucet with running water. That was very luxurious in those days.

"No namby-pamby now," said their nanny, Phoebe, every morning.

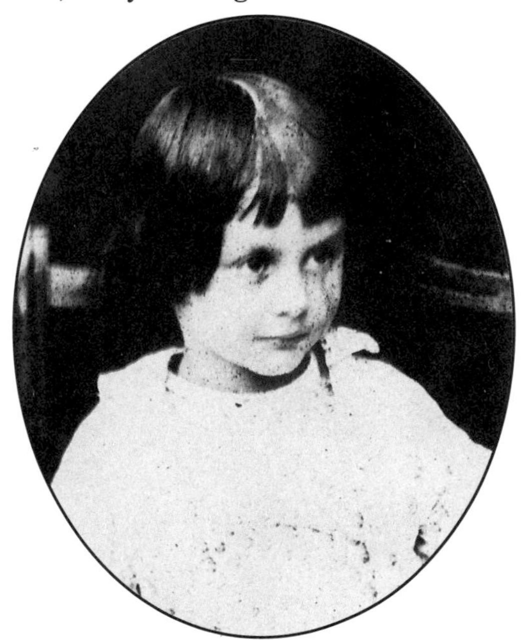

The first (sharp) photograph of Alice

The girls knew what that meant: they had to get into an ice-cold bath. (Too bad they didn't have warm water.)

Ina's cat, Dinah (the sister of poor Willikens), was forced to take a cold bath as well.

"No namby-pamby now," said Ina as she put the hissing, scratching Dinah into the bath.

When Alice was four years old, she thought Mr. Dodgson was a pest. He always wanted her to sit still for a picture. Alice could never sit still, so the pictures were always blurry. It wasn't until she was four and a half that she began to sharpen up. More or less.

Harry, Alice's big brother, was the first one to appear in a sharp picture. He was also the first to discover how much fun Mr. Dodgson was. Harry followed him around like a little puppy. Imagine, a grownup who actually listened to what you said, and treated you like an important person! And Mr. Dodgson told stories, played games, drew pictures, and did puzzles. (Some of them turned out to be *math* puzzles, but Harry hardly noticed.)

The first years it was mostly Harry and Ina who spent time with Mr. Dodgson. Later Alice was allowed to join them. When Harry got older, he was sent away to boarding school; then he saw Mr. Dodgson only during school vacations. What a pity, thought Harry. Lovely, thought Edith, who got to take his place. But little sister Rhoda was still too young — for a while, anyway.

Alice had had another brother, Arthur. But he died of scarlet fever when Alice was only a year old; she didn't remember him at all.

Alice's father was a very busy man. But Alice discovered she could go into the room where he kept his appointment book, look up a day (Tuesday, for example), write: GO RIDING WITH ALICE, and quite often it would happen.

Harry had his own pony, named Tommy. But since he didn't live at home any longer, the girls got to ride it. Their father's driver, Bultitude, had been kind enough to teach Alice to ride.

Alice and her father often rode in Christ Church Meadow, the large field next to the college. Her father taught Alice the names of all the trees and the birds they saw there and along the river Isis. They would get off their horses and look at flowers and insects. Alice's father knew them all.

And he could draw, too. He would sit, lost in thought, drawing figures on his blotting paper. He arranged for Alice to learn to draw and paint with water-colors.

One more thing about Alice's father: every day, at exactly noon, he would sneeze. Now, how many dads do you know who do that!

Alice's father sneezed every day at noon

The Poor Pitiful Dodo Bird

One day a messenger arrived with a letter from Mr. Dodgson. It said: *"Would Ina, Alice, and Edith like to go to the University Museum and look at something that doesn't exist?"*

"It must be something in the ghost room," said Alice, who had been to the museum before with Mr. Dodgson. There he had shown her an actual human skeleton. It was the skeleton of Giles Freeman Covington, who had been hanged March 17, 1791. Alice felt almost sorry for him, since he had never had a proper burial like other people, but had to stand there in the museum all the time.

The dodo painting by John Savery (1651) in the University Museum

"I don't want to see a ghost room," said Edith.

"No, we shall look at something else entirely," said Mr. Dodgson.

And there they were, in front of the impressive museum, big as a cathedral, with turrets and towers and a glass roof. It was Oxford's newest treasure.

They walked through the great hall filled with animal exhibits and skeletons.

"Some people say that, at midnight, all the animals in here come alive," said Mr. Dodgson.

"We'll be gone by then, won't we?" asked Edith.

"Now, let's see," said Mr. Dodgson, stopping in front of a small glass case. "This has got to be the most *remarkable* thing in the entire museum."

But what was it? The girls were disappointed. A little pile of brown stuff, a shapeless lump, and a more stretched-out . . .

"That," said Mr. Dodgson, "is a DODO."

"But doesn't a dodo look like that bird in the painting over there?" said Ina.

Hanging on the wall was an oil painting of a large fat bird with a giant bill and big feet. Only its wings were tiny and pitiful.

"That's right," said Mr. Dodgson. "But this one is the *real* dodo. If you'd like, I can tell you the true, sad story of the *real* dodo."

"Yes!" said Ina and Edith.

"Is it very sad?" asked Alice.

"Yes, it is, sadder than sad," said Mr. Dodgson.

"Then I'll cover my ears when the sad part starts," said Alice.

"Once upon a time," Mr. Dodgson began (as he always did), "a large and fat and happy bird strolled around a swamp all by herself on a desert island. (The island, which is called Mauritius, is located in the Indian Ocean.)

"It occurred to the dodo that she really ought to return to her nest and take over for her mate, who was sitting on their only egg.

"Mauritius was a beautiful island. The dodo had no natural enemies — not animal, reptile, or human. There were huge rain forests with ebony trees, orchids, and ferns. Lots of parrots and other birds sang up in the trees.

"But the dodo kept to the ground, since she couldn't fly. She didn't need to, either; there was plenty for her to eat where she was."

"What did the dodo eat?" asked Alice, who still hadn't needed to cover her ears.

"I honestly don't know," said Mr. Dodgson. "But it must have been something requiring a big strong bill. Perhaps she ate nuts from the *tambalocoque* tree.

"But then one day (remember, this was a long time ago, in the 1600s) a Dutch ship sailed toward Mauritius. Some sailors rowed ashore. Soon our dodo would see her first human being.

"When she heard voices, she became curious and went nearer. She got so excited she cried: 'Do-do, do-do.' Her mate and several other dodo birds came running.

"The hungry sailors captured all the dodoes and carried them on board the ship. The ship's dog discovered the nest with the dodo egg, and immediately bit it open and ate it up.

"'That fattest one,' said the cook, pointing at the dodo's mate, 'I'll cook for dinner tonight. It will be enough for the whole crew.'

"So that's how the dodo's egg became dog food, the dodo's mate became the sailors' dinner, and the dodo herself became a prisoner on board ship. Many days and nights passed. The dodo birds became very unhappy. They stopped eating and drinking. Some of them died, and others were cooked and eaten for dinner.

"When the ship reached Holland, all the birds were dead, except for our dodo. But, Alice, weren't you going to cover your ears?"

Alice, whose eyes were glazed over by this time, had completely forgotten to cover her ears.

"What happened then?" she whispered. "You must let it end happily."

"No," said Mr. Dodgson. "You'll have to cover your ears."

"It's too late now," said Alice.

"Yes," said Mr. Dodgson. "And it was too late

for the dodo as well. Too late for *all* dodoes. Only this particular one managed to survive long enough to be taken to London and put in a zoo. There she died of a broken heart.

"But someone arranged to have her body stuffed, and eventually she ended up with Elias Ashmole in Oxford, at the Ashmolean Museum. There she stood day in and day out. Until 1755, when it was discovered that she had lice. To keep them from spreading to all the other animals, it was decided that the dodo should be burned. The only things they saved were her head and left foot . . . They are now preserved here at the University Museum."

The girls raced back to the glass case. There! There was their dodo! A *head* and a *foot*!

"But I still haven't come to the saddest part of all," said Mr. Dodgson. "The sadder than sad part . . ."

"I can't stand any more," sniffed Alice.

"Dodo birds had lived many thousands of years in peace and harmony on their island. But after the first human arrived, it took less than two hundred years for the last dodo to die. Man exterminated the dodo. Once the last bird was dead, there was no way to ever bring them back."

"Stupid people!" said Edith.

"I should think they could have saved a few," said Ina.

"Why did those sailors ever have to find the dodo's island!" Alice sighed.

"Unfortunately, they also found Réunion, the white dodo's island, and the island of Rodrigues with its dodo, the solitaire. All the dodoes were exterminated, but from the bones scientists saw that the dodo was a relative of the pigeon. It was a giant pigeon that couldn't fly."

"I should rather have guessed an ostrich," said Ina. "They can't fly either, you know."

"No one today knows exactly what the dodo looked like, but that picture was painted before the stuffed dodo was burned up, and it was the *only* stuffed dodo in the world! And now you've seen the *only* dodo head in the entire world (the others are just sculls)."

"What good is that, when there aren't any more dodoes." Alice sighed and blew her nose.

"Not much, really," said Mr. Dodgson. "But you did get to see something that doesn't exist anymore, and you got to hear a story."

"But it was such a sad story," said Alice.

And so they went home.

That night Alice dreamed that she was in the museum at midnight. There, under the painting, was the dodo, alive and in person.

"Forgive us, please," said Alice, "for making you extinct."

"Oh, that's quite all right," said the dodo. "Besides, it wasn't really your fault."

"But it feels like it," said Alice.

"Let's hope that you humans learn something from your mistakes," said the dodo.

"Oh yes, we promise," said Alice.

Then the dodo came up and put a beautiful dodo egg in Alice's pinafore.

"Oh, thank you ever so much," said Alice respectfully. "I shall take good care of it. I promise."

Afterward, Alice wondered if it was really a dream. Perhaps it was more like a wish.

Doesn't Alice Go to School?

"Pricks, I must tell you something very sad," Alice told her governess the next morning. (Her real name was Miss Prickett.)

"Goodness me, whatever has happened?" said Miss Prickett, horrified.

"Well," said Alice. "This is so horrible, but the last dodo is, in fact, dead. And now there can never again be any dodo birds. *Ever.*"

"Oh," said Miss Prickett. "Is that all . . ."

"All!" said Alice. "Is that *all*!"

"Come along, girls," said Miss Prickett. "It's time for geography."

"Oh yes, geography," said Alice. "Let's read about the island of Mauritius!"

"But, my dear Alice," said Miss Prickett, "we are studying the geography of England."

And she hung a map of England on the wall in the nursery. The *nursery*? Yes, that's right. Ina, Alice, and Edith didn't go to school, although their brother Harry did. That was very common then. Boys went to school, and girls were educated at home by a governess.

Ina was Miss Prickett's favorite, because she always paid attention and studied her lessons properly. Alice asked too many questions (often questions that Miss Prickett couldn't answer). And sometimes Alice forgot to pay attention — like just now, when she ran up to the window to look at a pigeon that was sitting on the sill.

"Pricks," said Alice, "did you know that the dodo was related to the pigeon?"

"My dear Alice," said Miss Prickett in a voice that showed she didn't mean the word "dear" at all. "Come here and point out England's rivers."

"Cherwell," said Alice. "And . . . Isis . . ."

She could remember only the two rivers that flowed through Oxford. Miss Prickett sighed and asked Ina instead. Of course Ina knew.

"Ina doesn't find the English rivers to be dull and dry," said Miss Prickett.

Alice started to giggle.

"What is it, Alice?" asked Miss Prickett.

"Of course she doesn't find them dull and dry," said Alice. "That was quite witty."

"Was it?" said Miss Prickett.

"Yes, because the English rivers could never be dull and dry!" said Alice.

Miss Prickett wasn't the only teacher the girls had. Since she wasn't very good at singing or French, the girls had other teachers for those subjects.

Later (when Alice was seventeen) she had an art teacher for drawing and painting. And not just any art teacher, but the famous artist and writer, John Ruskin.

If Ina was Miss Prickett's favorite, then Alice was John Ruskin's. Alice liked to draw and John Ruskin thought she had talent. He would lend her his own paintings to copy, and sometimes those of his late friend J. M. W. Turner.

Just then someone knocked on the nursery door. It was Mr. Dodgson.

"Mr. Dodgson," said Alice, "Ina doesn't think that the English rivers are dull and dry."

"Is that so?" said Mr. Dodgson. "Perhaps she's right. It would be quite difficult to row down a dull and dry river. Instead, I suggest that you come down to the garden and have your picture taken."

"Have you asked Mrs. Liddell?" said Miss Prickett.

"Yes," said Mr. Dodgson, "and she has said yes."

"Hurrah!" cried Alice (for even if it was boring to pose for pictures, it was much better than the English rivers).

Alice as a Beggar Girl . . .

it here on the grass," Mr. Dodgson said from behind his camera. "Ina in the middle."

"We can pretend that I'm sleeping," said Alice, laying her head in Ina's lap. (Alice knew that it was easier to hold still if you pretended to be asleep.)

Mrs. Liddell came down into the garden with her coat and hat on. She was off to pay a visit to someone. Bultitude had already brought the horse and carriage.

"Oh, what wrinkled dresses!" she said. "See that the girls have something clean and pressed. And no pinafores."

"Shall they wear their new frocks with the ruffled sleeves?" asked Phoebe.

"Yes," said Mrs. Liddell.

"But you must hurry," Mr. Dodgson told the girls. "The light is perfect for a picture right now." Alice was the first to be ready, because her hair was so easy to comb. Ina and Edith had a more difficult time.

Most girls then had long hair that was curled with curling papers or a curling iron, but Mrs. Liddell thought Alice looked far better in short, straight hair, with bangs, even though that was unusual.

"We'll start with you, Alice," said Mr. Dodgson. "Please stand over there against the wall."

"I shall have to think of something dull," said Alice, "while you count to 42."

"Think of the English rivers," said Mr. Dodgson.

Mr. Dodgson developed the glass plate in a little room in the Liddells' basement. He had already put his tank and bottles and other supplies there.

Poor Edith! Her dress was in the ironing basket, and it would take too long to press it. So she had to go back up to the nursery with Miss Prickett. Ina came down wearing her new dress and hat.

"*Must* I wear a hat?" whined Alice.

Mr. Dodgson promised Alice they would take a dress-up picture of her later, if she would only agree to wear a hat. And so she did, of course.

. . . and as Mother Likes Her

They weren't allowed to sit on the grass in their new dresses, so Alice sat on the seesaw instead, and Ina stood beside her.

"Why should it be so terrible to get a little bit dirty?" said Alice, sighing.

"When we are done here, you can dress up as a little beggar girl," said Mr. Dodgson, "and get as dirty as you'd like."

"Yes!" said Alice. "We can pretend that I'm the Little Match Girl!"

Then Alice thought about that sad, sad story by Hans Christian Andersen. How she had cried when Mr. Dodgson had read it to her!

"Forty-two!" Mr. Dodgson shouted, and then it was time for the plate to be developed.

Ina had had enough posing for one day, but Alice ran down to the basement to get an old ragged nightgown.

"Do I look poor now?" Alice wondered.

"We should probably rip it up a bit more," said Mr. Dodgson. "And it's much too clean."

Alice rolled around in the grass. She rubbed dirt into the gown. She climbed up the big chestnut tree.

"Now what?" asked Alice. "Oh yes, the Little Match Girl had bare feet."

Alice pulled off her shoes and stockings.

"Ouch! The gravel hurts my feet," she said. "It's not that easy to be poor . . ."

Mr. Dodgson got a little rug for Alice to stand on.

"Does it look as if I'm standing barefoot in the snow?"

"Well, not exactly."

"I look poor and hungry, at least?" said Alice.

"Oh, absolutely," agreed Mr. Dodgson.

"But then I am angry as well," said Alice. "It's terribly unfair that I should have to freeze to death on New Year's Eve, just when everyone else is sitting inside eating roast goose . . ."

"Good!" cried Mr. Dodgson. "Just like that!"

Looking angry for a full forty-two seconds wasn't easy, but Alice managed to do it.

As quickly as possible, Alice changed out of her beggar clothes. She put on her dress and shoes and stockings, and had just finished tying her pinafore strings when her mother came home.

Nightcap (winter)

Chemise

Stockings with garters

Petticoats. In winter, the middle one was made of flannel

Pantalets

Striped stockings

Garter

Parasol

4
8
10
12
14
16

Girls wore different skirt lengths, depending on their age

Nightgown

Camisole

Pinafore for everyday use

Alice's Elegant Clothes

Alice and her sisters were always well dressed — every single day. You can see that in Mr. Dodgson's pictures.

In those days, people hardly ever bought clothes ready-made. Alice's mother traveled to London, where she bought fabrics and fashion magazines. Then a seamstress came and made clothes for everyone except Alice's father. (His were made by a tailor in Oxford.)

The seamstress always made three identical dresses: one for Ina, one for Alice, and one for Edith. The girls never wore hand-me-downs.

Mrs. Liddell decided what the dresses would look like; they were always the latest fashion.

Alice's mother

Summer dresses were usually made of white cotton with frills, embroidery, and lace. Winter dresses were more colorful.

The seamstress made their underwear, too, full of lace, embroidery, frills, and tiny pleats.

Alice thought it was hard to keep her white dresses clean. Fortunately, every Monday, washerwomen came to do the laundry. They washed the clothes by hand down in the cellar.

It took hours to iron all the frills, pleats, lace, and embroidered edging. There was no electricity to heat the iron; it was warmed on top of a wood stove or iron range. Or the iron was heated with glowing charcoal inside.

Alice's mother was famous for her beautiful clothes. Every morning her maid would help her lace her corset and pull it in; it was important to have a small waist. When Mrs. Liddell was expecting a baby (and that was rather often), she would never want to be seen in public.

To make her long skirts stand out, Mrs. Liddell wore layers of petticoats and sometimes a crinoline (a kind of steel-cage underskirt).

Luckily for her daughters, Mrs. Liddell was too modern to make them wear corsets or crinolines. But they *always* had to wear hats and gloves when they went out.

But not all children had such elegant clothes as did Alice . . .

A most unusual picture by Mr. Dodgson of Coates, the daughter of one of his father's servants

Ordinary Children Lived Differently

The Liddell family belonged to the English upper class. Dean Liddell earned so much money that the family could afford elegant clothes, books, toys, and teachers for the children. They had a beautiful home, gave big parties, and had lots of servants. Seamstresses and servants earned very little money. They got their rooms, meals,

Children had to help with the harvest or tend animals

This drawing, from the 1842 Mines Report, shows a girl pulling a wagon of coal through a narrow tunnel

and a little cash. Their children seldom went to school, not even the boys. Clothes were handed down from older brothers or sisters or other relatives. Poor children didn't own books, and if they had toys, they would have been homemade.

Children helped their parents with work. If the father was a baker, the children would deliver bread to customers. If the parents worked on a farm, the children helped in the fields or took care of the cows and sheep. Children who lived in town went around selling such things as matches.

Some children had to do heavy work. They worked as miners or chimney sweeps, as their small size allowed them to squeeze into tight spaces. Many children worked in textile mills; their quick, small fingers were needed to knot the broken threads.

Poor children never played with rich children. One reason was, they never met at school. We can be sure that poor children would have looked longingly at Alice and her sisters when they were out with Miss Prickett or Mr. Dodgson.

Alice probably never thought much about it. Of course, she knew that there were "poor children," but most likely she couldn't have imagined how they actually lived. And the Little Match Girl was only a story, wasn't it?

Young girls often sold flowers, even late at night outside theaters or inside restaurants

Girls earned only about 30 cents a week selling matches, which was often a cover-up for begging

An Adventure in the Botanic Garden

Do I have everything now? Alice wondered to herself. Nuts and cakes for the monkeys, bread for the ducks, sketchbook, pen, the hat with the pretty blue silk band . . .

Today there would be no lessons; instead, they were allowed to go with Mr. Dodgson to the Botanic Garden, not far from Christ Church.

"I think we should take the High," said Alice.

"Dead Man's Walk is closer," said Ina. "Or do you think we might meet a ghost?"

"Not in the daytime," said Alice. "Don't be so silly."

"Is it because of the snails?" asked Mr. Dodgson.

Alice sighed. It *was* because of the snails. They were usually on the wall by Merton College. Alice's flesh crawled just thinking about them.

"If only you got to know some snails, you'd get used to them," said Mr. Dodgson.

And so they took Dead Man's Walk, anyway. Mr. Dodgson stopped and picked up a snail. Ugh.

"This reminds me of a snail I once knew," he said. "I had two of them, Misch and Masch, at the

Mr. Dodgson, as a boy, with his snails

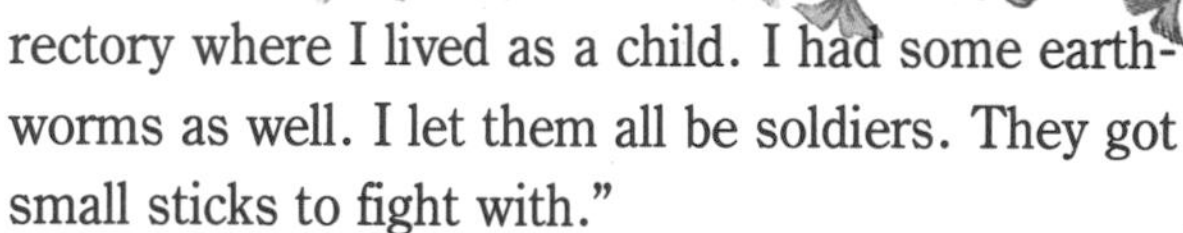

rectory where I lived as a child. I had some earthworms as well. I let them all be soldiers. They got small sticks to fight with."

"Did they really fight?" asked Ina.

"No, they turned out to be pacifists, peace-lovers, the whole lot. They wouldn't even stand guard. They just crawled away. So I gave up."

Now they were past the snail wall. Alice thought it was much nicer feeding the ducks in the river Cherwell. Soon all the bread was gone.

"I had planned to introduce you to *Ginkgo biloba* today," said Mr. Dodgson.

"Who is that?" said Edith.

"The world's oldest tree," said Mr. Dodgson. "Many millions of years old!"

"But," said Ina. "The oldest tree in the Garden is the yew that Bobart planted in about 1650."

"Sorry, I meant the world's oldest *kind* of tree," said Mr. Dodgson. "Ginkgo trees were found on earth long before other kinds of broad-leaf trees — even during the dinosaur era."

"What a bumpy little tree," said Alice.

"This particular tree was planted here around 1800; the seeds probably came all the way from China. The gingko isn't related to any other broad-leaf tree. Look at the leaves," said Mr. Dodgson. "The veins start down at the stem and then spread out like a fan. No other leaf looks like that."

"Oh, I must draw one," said Alice.

"It would be easier to take one and press it," said Mr. Dodgson.

"May I?" asked Alice.

"Yes," said Mr. Dodgson. "In the interest of science."

Alice pressed a leaf between two pages of her sketchbook.

"Doesn't it have any relatives at all?" asked Ina.

"No," said Mr. Dodgson. "All of its relatives died out when the earth became colder and ice moved down from the north. But in China the ginkgo managed to move far enough south to survive the Ice Age. When humans arrived, they helped by planting ginkgo trees. In China the ginkgo is thought to protect against fire, and it's considered a sacred tree.

"This particular tree is a male. In order to produce seeds, he must have a female tree nearby, so he can blow his pollen over to her."

"Where is the female tree?" asked Ina.

"There isn't any," said Mr. Dodgson.

"Poor ginkgo!" said Alice. "No family, and no wife! Here, you may have my blue silk hatband."

The ginkgo leaf that Alice pressed

The only thing now that could cheer Alice up was Professor Daubeny's monkeys. The professor was head of the Botanic Garden and a good friend of Mr. Dodgson and the girls. He would tell stories about the Old Days at the Garden. (If you want to read about Bobart's Beard, the Dead Rat, or the Weed That Ran Away, look at page 41.) The monkeys were in their cage now, but Alice knew they were allowed to come out and join the guests whenever Professor Daubeny had a party. And once, years ago, Professor Buckland had brought a live bear, dressed as a Christ Church student, to one of the parties.

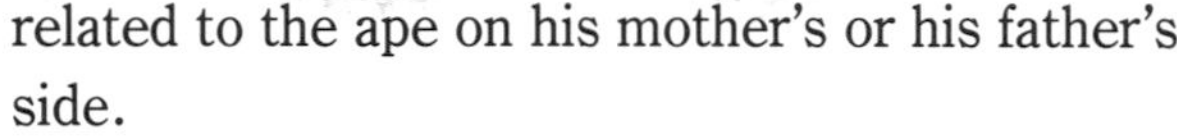

The girls were busy feeding the monkeys nuts and cakes when Professor Daubeny walked by.

"It's a good thing you are kind to your relatives," he said.

"I've heard something about that," said Alice. "But is it true that we are related to apes?"

"It depends on whom you ask," said Mr. Dodgson. "Bishop Wilberforce believes that man descended from Adam and Eve."

"But I agree with Mr. Darwin and Mr. Huxley," said the professor. "Man descended from animals, and our closest relative is the ape."

"But Grandmother is even closer," said Edith.

"You're right about that," said the professor. "It reminds me of the heated debate after Mr. Huxley's talk at the museum. A woman fainted, and the bishop asked Mr. Huxley if he was related to the ape on his mother's or his father's side.

"Does Mr. Huxley look like an ape?" asked Edith.

"Of course not," said Alice. "You don't understand — we humans are rather like apes."

"Not our hair," said Ina, "or our feet."

"I wish I had feet like an ape," said Alice. "They seem much better than our silly feet."

"Now you must visit *Nymphaea daubenyana,*" said the professor. "The water lily that is named after me. And *Victoria* too. Soon the pads will be so large a baby could float on them!"

Like Thumbelina, Alice thought. When Mr. Dodgson had read her Hans Christian Andersen's story, Alice had wished she could float on a lily pad, too. But she was much too big.

Professor Daubeny with one of his monkeys

"*Why* does one always have to get so frightfully big?" asked Alice.

"I ask myself the same thing," said Mr. Dodgson.

"What if we could shrink?" said Alice.

"Try it," said Mr. Dodgson. "Perhaps if you ate a bit of cake . . ."

"The cakes are all gone," said Alice

And then it was time to go home. Too bad, but at least they would get to walk up the High. Alice liked window shopping much better than looking at snails.

As usual, they said hello to Mr. Theophilus Carter, who was standing in the doorway of his furniture shop, wearing a top hat. Alice knew that he had invented an "alarm-clock bed" that would toss a sleeping person out on the floor. It had been shown at the Great Exhibition in 1851!

They stopped at Boffin's to buy cakes; Alice wanted to see if they would make her shrink. They didn't, even though she ate four of them.

"Are you coming to play croquet with us tomorrow?" Alice asked.

"With pleasure," said Mr. Dodgson. "But it's best if we ask your mother first."

What the Professor told:

Bobart's Beard

In 1642, Jacob Bobart became the Botanic Garden's first gardener. He was dirty and grubby and had a beard down to his waist. And he had a pet goat that was his constant companion.

One day an absentminded and somewhat confused man visited the Garden. When he saw Bobart's beard, he grabbed it and pulled, shouting, "Help! Help! Bobart has eaten his horse and the tail is sticking out of his mouth!"

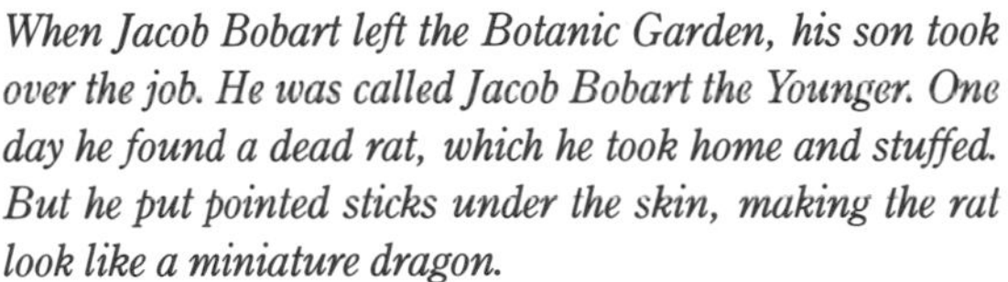

The Dead Rat

When Jacob Bobart left the Botanic Garden, his son took over the job. He was called Jacob Bobart the Younger. One day he found a dead rat, which he took home and stuffed. But he put pointed sticks under the skin, making the rat look like a miniature dragon.

Educated men came to have a look. They were impressed, convinced that Bobart had discovered a whole new animal species.

The Weed That Ran Away

In the 1700s, a professor brought some seeds back from Mount Etna in Italy, and planted them in his garden. What came up was a plant that was later called Oxford ragwort (Senecio squalidus *in Latin).*

It grew out of the garden and up over the wall. It kept on growing, climbing wall after wall, until it had gone all the way to the railway station.

There it discovered that it liked the roadbeds best of all. The suction created by the trains passing helped spread the seeds, and soon it had grown all the way to London.

Today Oxford ragwort, usually called groundsel, is one of England's most common weeds.

See what mischief a few tiny seeds can make!

The Best Number Is

When Mr. Dodgson arrived the next day, Alice was sitting in the garden, sketching the big chestnut tree. As usual, Dinah, the cat, had climbed up on one of the branches. But just as Alice started to draw her, Dinah would tease her by moving over to another branch, or by disappearing behind a cover of leaves.

"You're driving me quite mad, Dinah," said Alice. "It's hard enough drawing all these leaves."

"May I have a look?" Mr. Dodgson asked. "It's rather exciting, with so many cats sitting in the same tree. Look at that one, where you only had time to draw her sneering grin . . ."

"Oh no, that was a mistake," said Alice. "Let's do something else. We'll think of numbers. You start."

"Seventy-four thousand and eighty-eight," said Mr. Dodgson.

"74,088?" said Alice. "I was certain you would choose 42. You always say that I should sit still for forty-two seconds, and that the diameter of Mercury* is exactly forty-two feet, and that if you fall down a rabbit hole, it will be exactly forty-two minutes before you reach the other side of the earth. (Is that really true, by the way?)"

"I haven't really tried," said Mr. Dodgson. "But I have worked it out. If you know the speed of the stone and the circumference of the earth, then . . ."

"All right," said Alice. "But there aren't such deep rabbit holes. What's so good about 74,088?"

"74,088 is built on 42," said Mr. Dodgson.

"If you take 42 blocks," he continued, "and put them in a row, and then put another 42 next to them, and another 42 next to them, and continue like that until you have 42 rows of 42 blocks, you will have a square made up of 1,764 blocks."

"I don't have that many blocks," said Alice.

"But we'll pretend that you do. Now put another layer of blocks on top of the first square, then another, and another, until . . ."

"Of course you want me to pile up 42 layers," said Alice.

"That's correct," said Mr. Dodgson. "Can you guess how many blocks you'll have then?"

"It wouldn't work," said Alice. "It would fall."

"Not if you pretend," said Mr. Dodgson, working it out in Alice's sketchbook. "42 × 42 × 42 . . ."

". . . is 74,088!" said Alice. "That's almost more 42 than 42 itself. But now it's my turn. Shall I tell you my number? Yes, I shall: 9."

"Why 9?" asked Mr. Dodgson.

"Because I'm nine years old," said Alice.

"But you'll be ten tomorrow," said Mr. Dodgson.

"Yes, and that's what is so very silly," said Alice. "Today is the last day of my whole life I can get by with just one number for my age. Imagine — my last day as a single number . . ."

"Poor you," said Mr. Dodgson. "Try growing backwards, instead."

"I've tried that," Alice said, "but it didn't work."

She drew a big 9 in her sketchbook.

"If I nail this 9 up on the tree, I can fool Dinah into going into the loop, and I can hang my coat on the hook. If it starts raining, I can put on my coat,

* The pond in the middle of Tom Quad, Christ Church.

turn the 9 upside down, and sit here without getting wet. Dinah won't get wet either, but we'll lose a 3."

"Is that so?" asked Mr. Dodgson.

"Oh yes, because 3 times 3 is 9," said Alice. "But a 6 has only room for 2 times 3."

"You're right about that," said Mr. Dodgson. "What magic! A 3 disappearing in a tree. But do you know what there is in my 42?"

"Well, 6 times 7," said Alice. "That makes 42."

"Not only that," said Mr. Dodgson, "but 3 times 14 . . ."

". . . and 2 times 21," said Alice.

"And 1 times 42," said Mr. Dodgson.

"But that was almost cheating," said Alice.

Just then, Ina came down to the garden.

"What are you doing?" she asked.

"Having a mathematics lesson," said Mr. Dodgson.

"We certainly are not!" said Alice. "I hate mathematics. We are just playing with numbers."

"I thought that was the same thing," said Mr. Dodgson.

Just then, it was teatime. And in spite of Alice's eating more cakes and biscuits than ever, she didn't shrink a single inch. Perhaps she even grew some! And the next day she became a double number. The only good thing, Mr. Dodgson told her, was that she could still show her age with her fingers. But this would be the last year for that as well.

An Outing in the Pouring Rain

Spring went, summer came; Alice was ten now, Ina thirteen, and Edith eight. They saw Mr. Dodgson almost every day. But Rhoda was still too little to join them.

"Mr. Dodgson is here all the time," said Mrs. Liddell. "I think it's beginning to be a bit much."

"We don't think so," said the girls.

"But people will begin to wonder," said Mrs. Liddell.

"What would they wonder about?" said Alice.

"People may imagine that Mr. Dodgson is fond of Miss Prickett," said Alice's mother.

"That was the silliest thing I've ever heard," said Alice. "We're the ones he's fond of."

"And now he's asked if we may row with him to Nuneham," said Ina. "Please, Mama . . ."

"There won't be room for Pricks," said Alice, "because Fanny and Elizabeth, his sisters, are going with us, and Mr. Duckworth."

"Well, then," said Mrs. Liddell, "if his sisters are going along . . ."

Tuesday and Thursday were Nuneham days, the days picnicking was allowed on Lord Harcourt's estate. He had even had small shelters built for the picnickers.

Fanny and Elizabeth were just slightly over thirty, but the girls considered them old. And what a lot of room they took up in the boat with all their petticoats and crinolines! Alice sat squeezed between them in the stern, manning the rudder.

At Nuneham, the girls jumped ashore and ran to a cottage to borrow plates and silverware. Mr. Duckworth unpacked the chicken, salad, and cakes from the picnic basket, while Mr. Dodgson boiled water for tea on a camp stove.

After their picnic, they hiked to the top of the highest hill to look at the view.

"Lord Harcourt had originally planned to build a ruin right here," said Mr. Dodgson.

"Can one *build* a ruin?" asked Ina. "Aren't ruins old buildings that have fallen apart?"

"Yes, they are," said Mr. Dodgson. "But Lord Harcourt wanted it to look just as it does outside of Rome. There are lots of ruins there. But for some reason, in the eighteenth century, the top of Carfax Conduit, the ancient Oxford water tower, ended up here instead. Now then, is it really only the top?"

Rowing home, they asked

each other riddles. Fanny and Elizabeth knew all the answers.

Finally Mr. Dodgson asked, "Why is a raven like a writing desk?"

"Too bad you didn't ask what the *difference* between them was," said Alice.

Just then, it began to rain. Mr. Dodgson and Mr. Duckworth started rowing with all their might. And then it began to pour. Everything was getting wet: hats, hair, skirts, petticoats.

"This will never do," said Mr. Dodgson. "We'll stop in Sandford and call at Mr. Ranken's house."

Mr. Ranken's landlady opened the door. She made a fire in the fireplace and hung their clothes up to dry. Fanny and Elizabeth and the Liddell girls waited, wrapped in blankets.

The men left to look for a horse-drawn cab; they didn't find one until they got as far as Iffley, more than a mile away.

Alice discovered that Fanny and Elizabeth were a lot more fun than she had thought.

"Tell about when you were children," begged Alice. "Was Mr. Dodgson a nice little brother?"

"Oh yes," said Elizabeth. "He was an expert in playing. He tried to train earthworms and —"

"— snails," said Alice. "What else did he do?"

"Do you remember the marionettes?" asked Fanny.

"And when the railway first came," said Elizabeth, "he made a train out of a wheelbarrow and a barrel . . ."

"And that other truck," said Fanny. "The one we were forced to ride in on the garden paths . . ."

"Do you remember his

Love's Railway Guide

(made up by Mr. Dodgson as a child)

Rule I. *All passengers when upset are requested to lie still until picked up – as it is requisite that at least three trains should go over them, to entitle them to the attention of the doctor and assistants.*

II. *If a passenger comes to a station after the train has passed the next (i.e. when it is about 100 m. off) he may not run after it but must wait for the next.*

III. *When a passenger has no money and still wants to go by the train, he must stop at whatever station he happened to be at, and earn money, by making tea for the station master (who drinks it at all hours of the day and night) and grinding sand for the company (what use they make of it they are* not *bound to explain).*

timetables? And his railway rules?" said Elizabeth.

"And the secret things under the nursery floor," said Fanny.

"What were they?" asked Alice.

But just then Mr. Dodgson arrived with the cab, and Alice never got to find out. They dressed quickly in their *almost* dry clothes and set off for home.

Alice completely forgot to ask about the secrets under the nursery floor; instead, she asked about something else:

"Why was a raven like a writing desk?"

"I haven't the foggiest idea," said Mr. Dodgson.

"That can't be the answer to a riddle," said Alice.

"But there are riddles in this world which, in fact, have no answers," said Mr. Dodgson.

Antipodes Croquet and a Little Green Door

After a couple of weeks, Alice said, "Mr. Dodgson, we were going to take another boating trip, to make up for the one that was rained out . . ."

"Yes," said Mr. Dodgson. "Why not tomorrow? It's even a Thursday like the last time."

But the next day it rained *again* and Mr. Dodgson was invited to the Liddells' for lunch. Perhaps it would clear up by afternoon. But it cleared up only long enough for a game of croquet in the garden. Dean Liddell and Mr. Duckworth joined them. As they were all playing, a hedgehog came trotting by. When Alice ran over to it, it rolled itself up in a little ball.

"Lucky for you," Alice said to the hedgehog, "that we didn't mistake you for a croquet ball."

"In the Antipodes they always play croquet with hedgehogs," said Mr. Dodgson.

"What are the Antipodes?" asked Edith.

"They are islands, so called because they lie on exactly the opposite side of the earth," he said.

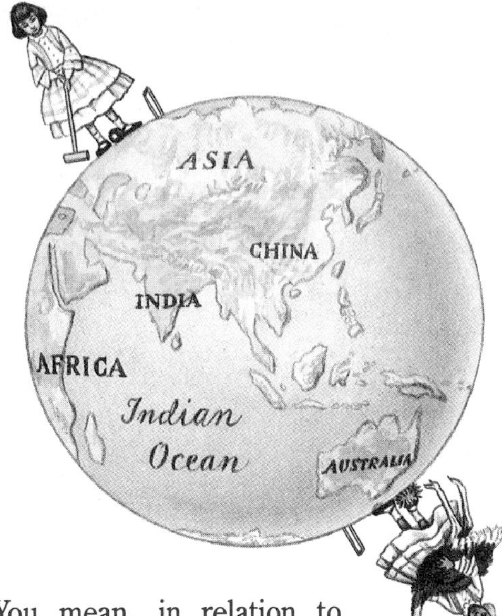

"You mean, in relation to England," said Ina (who, of course, was good at geography).

"What do they call us, then?" asked Alice.

"That's a good question," said Mr. Dodgson.

"They call us England, of course," said Ina.

"The word 'antipodes' comes from the Greek *anti,* which means 'against,' and *podes,* which means 'feet,'" said Dean Liddell, who knew Greek. "They walk with their feet against ours."

"However, there's a bit of space between," said Mr. Duckworth.

"Yes, forty-two minutes," said Alice.

"Exactly," said Mr. Dodgson. "Haven't you ever heard of the Antipodes? And Antipodes croquet?"

"No," said Alice. "But if they use hedgehogs for balls, what do they use for mallets?"

"Ostriches," said Mr. Dodgson. "And sometimes flamingos. But they're difficult to play with, and the balls are always running away."

"Like this one," said Alice. "Where did it go?"

"It ran over to the door," said Edith.

Alice ran after it, over to the little green door in the garden wall.

"Can't we open the door?" said Alice.

"No," said her father. "You know very well that the green door is always locked. You're not allowed to go in there. Our garden ends here."

Yes, Alice knew that. She had always wondered what was behind that door. Little locked doors were certainly annoying . . .

"Well, tomorrow we shall row upriver," said Mr. Dodgson. "At least then we'll see what there is there. If it doesn't rain, that is."

"But of course tomorrow is Friday," said Ina, "and so there is no reason to row to Nuneham."

Then it started raining again. Mr. Dodgson invited Mr. Duckworth to join him for dinner. That evening he wrote in his diary: "*I mark this day with a white stone,*" because it had been most enjoyable, in spite of the rain.

What's behind the little green door?

The Golden Afternoon

It rained all that night and the next morning as well. Alice wished so hard it would stop that it actually did. And then it became gloriously warm and sunny, instead. The grass dried quickly.

Alice jumped down into the rowboat they had rented at Salters' at Folly Bridge.

"Please, Mr. Dodgson," she said, "tell us a story! And a really l-o-n-g one."

"Oh yes, please!" said Ina and Edith.

"But, dear Prima, Secunda, and Tertia" (he sometimes called Ina, Alice, and Edith that), "shouldn't we save the story for our picnic?"

"No, start the story *now*!" they all said.

And so he did. And everyone who has ever heard that story knows that it became something very *special.* (And those who have read the first chapter of this book know, too, so we aren't going to tell you about it again.)

The day after Mr. Dodgson told that fantastic story (did it ever really end?), Alice and her family took the 9:02 train to London. The girls got to go along so they could see the Great Exhibition. (Not that one with the alarm-clock bed, that was 1851, but the new one that was held in 1862.)

At the station they met Mr. Dodgson. He was on his way to London to go to the theater, and to meet Fanny and Elizabeth. Alice reminded him about writing down the story.

"Well," said Mr. Dodgson, "we shall see."

But he did go and sit in another carriage, where he began planning how he would go about dividing the story into chapters. Then he wrote down what each chapter would be called.

After a couple of days he ran into the Liddells at the Great Exhibition.

"Well," said Alice. "Have you started?"

Alice kept at him every time they met, which was rather often.

Sometimes they went up to Mr. Dodgson's rooms, where they listened to stories or sang the girls' favorite song, "Sally, Come Up." Sometimes Mr. Dodgson came to their house and

helped them with their scrapbooks or played another kind of croquet, which he invented himself: Castle Croquet.

They made several outings. Once Ida and Margaret (Chemistry Professor Brodie's daughters) went with them.

This is what Mr. Dodgson wrote in his diary on the sixth of August:

Harcourt and I took the three Liddells up to Godstow, where we had tea; we tried the game of "the Ural Mountains" on the way, but it did not prove very successful, and I had to go on with my interminable fairy-tale of Alice's Adventures. *We got back soon after eight, and had supper in my rooms, the children coming over for a short while. A very enjoyable expedition — the last, I should think, to which Ina is likely to be allowed to come — her fourteenth time.*

Indeed, the next day, when Mr. Dodgson walked across Tom Quad, he met two horse-drawn cabs loaded down with the whole Liddell family (including the servants). They were going to their summer house at Llandudno, in Wales, far from Oxford. It would be months before they would return.

"We'll meet in the autumn," cried Alice. "Don't forget to write down the story . . ."

A Dull Autumn . . .

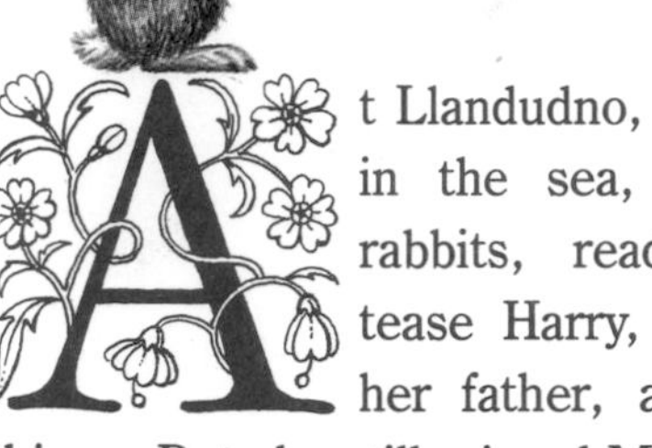

At Llandudno, Alice could swim in the sea, search for wild rabbits, read, write letters, tease Harry, take walks with her father, and lots of other things. But she still missed Mr. Dodgson.

He spent a good deal of his vacation at Croft Rectory, in Yorkshire, with his father (his mother had died long before) and all ten of his brothers and sisters. He had his camera with him and took pictures of his family and friends.

It was the middle of October before he and the Liddells were all back in Oxford again.

"May we invite Mr. Dodgson?" asked Alice.

"No," said her mother. "The seamstress is coming today."

It was like that every day. If it wasn't a seamstress, it was a guest or a visit to make.

When Mr. Dodgson asked to borrow the pictures for tinting, Mrs. Liddell said no. He didn't dare ask if the girls could take a walk with him. And he was getting nowhere with the story.

Finally Alice asked, "Why can't we see Mr. Dodgson?"

"It's not proper," said her mother. "A girl Ina's age mustn't spend time with single men. Besides, she's beginning to get bored with your outings."

"But Edith and I could certainly . . ." said Alice.

"And I," said Rhoda.

"You are too little," said Alice.

"One is always too little," said Rhoda, sighing. "Or too big."

In the middle of November, Alice accidentally ran into Mr. Dodgson out on Tom Quad.

"Oh, Mr. Dodgson!!!" shouted Alice from across the quad, as she ran toward him (she forgot shouting was forbidden). Maybe she had planned to give him a big hug, but she heard Pricks call and she stopped.

"How are you?" she asked politely, instead. "And how is the story coming?"

"Oh yes, *that* . . ." Mr. Dodgson hesitated. "Yes . . . it will most likely be ready by Christmas."

And *just then* he decided to get back to work on the story, since Alice wanted it so much. And *right then* Alice decided to ask her mother, one more time, just in case. And believe it or not, she said yes! And the following week Mr. Dodgson found a note in his mailbox:

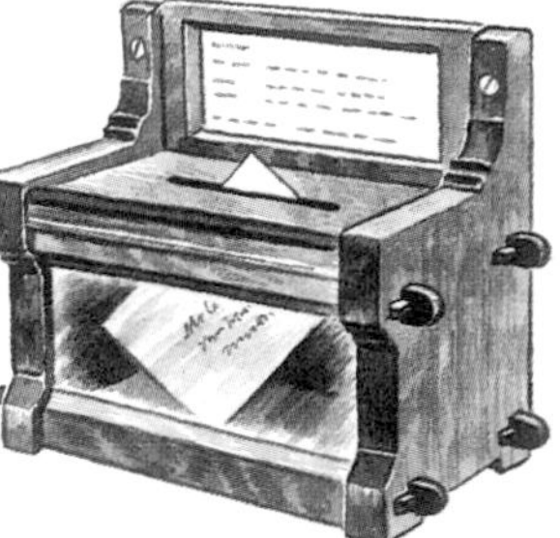

Dear Mr. Dodgson,
May Alice and Edith come to call, or would you prefer to come here for tea?
Respectfully,
Mrs. H. G. Liddell

So Mr. Dodgson came for tea, and everything was normal again. Mrs. Liddell wasn't around, but that was because she was expecting a baby soon. In those days, ladies kept out of sight when they were pregnant. And Ina was in bed with a bad cold.

When they finished their tea, Mr. Dodgson

. . . That Got Better

helped the girls with the scrapbooks* that he had given them. And when Alice had shown him her drawings and told him about the wild rabbits, she remembered that she hadn't asked Mr. Dodgson what he did on his vacation.

"This and that," he said. "Sometimes everything possible."

"Even backwards," Alice added. "But say what you really did."

"I took some pictures," he said. "Would you like to see?" He took out his album.

"This girl is also named Alice. Alice Donkin. Here we're pretending that she's running away."

Alice thought she looked silly, that Alice Donkin, but she didn't say so. Instead, she said, "Well, then, I think we should play Doublets."

It was a game Mr. Dodgson had made up.

"Yes," he said. "We'll turn *dog* into *cat*."

"May I play, too?" asked Rhoda.

"You have to know the alphabet to play Doublets," said Alice. "And you don't."

"I shall learn those silly letters," Rhoda said, "and then I'll be big enough, only not *too* big."

"No, don't be too big," said Mr. Dodgson.

How to Play Doublets

Choose two words with the same number of letters. Write them one under the other, with some space in between. Change one letter at a time in the word on top until you have turned it into the word on the bottom. Each time it has to be a real word (or name) "that can be used in good society," as Mr. Dodgson said. No misspelled or made-up words. Sometimes it's hard and you may have to take the "long way round" before you get it right.

The one who uses the fewest words to get there wins. Like this: DOG, *dot, cot,* CAT. *Try to make* BREAD *from* FLOUR. *Or* FOUR *into* FIVE. *Or ... make one up yourself.*

DOG
DOT
COT
CAT

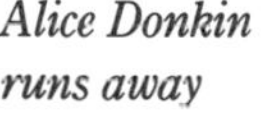

Alice Donkin runs away

** What did the girls collect? There were old family coats of arms that they cut out of letterheads or calling cards. The Liddell family had lions on its coat of arms (that explains why there were lions on the Lexicon Staircase). Mrs. Liddell's family had a unicorn on its coat of arms; Alice spent a lot of time looking at it. Even if people said that unicorns didn't exist, she still hoped they did.*

The Telescope and Tom Tower

Mr. Dodgson printed the story in ink, leaving space for the pictures. He finished it at Croft over the Christmas holidays. Then he tried to illustrate it. How hard it was! He had often drawn pictures for his stories, but on small pieces of paper that were thrown out later. These drawings would be saved! He borrowed Dean Liddell's zoology book to see what the animals in his story really looked like.

Mr. Dodgson's own sketches of Alice playing croquet in the story

He saw the girls now and then, but if Ina came along, Miss Prickett always did, too. Harry, however, could have breakfast at Mr. Dodgson's all by himself if he wanted to (whenever he was home during school vacations).

One evening the girls and Miss Prickett went to visit Mr. Dodgson to look at the stars.

"We'll see them best from the roof," he said.

"Is one allowed on the roof?" asked Ina.

"Only in the interest of science," said Mr. Dodgson.

The sky was dark, but crystal-clear. While Mr. Dodgson set up the telescope, the girls sang:

Twinkle, twinkle, little star,
How I wonder what you are!

"How many stars are there?" Edith asked.

"So many even I can't count that high," said Mr. Dodgson. "With a larger telescope, you would see even more. And behind them are still more. And behind them. And behind them . . ."

"Where does it all end, then?" asked Alice.

"It never ends," said Mr. Dodgson. "The universe goes on for all eternity."

"But it must end somewhere," said Alice.

"No," said Mr. Dodgson. "But since everything here on earth ends, we can't understand what eternity is. We've never experienced it."

"Yes, we have," said Alice. "In church. One must sit there an eternity . . ."

(Alice and her sisters went to church several times a week. They sat quietly in Christ Church Cathedral below Dean Liddell's chair.)

"Take a good book along next time," said Mr. Dodgson (who was against children being bored in church). "Then your 'eternity' will go faster."

It was nine o'clock. The church bells of Oxford were ringing, except for those of Christ Church. By tradition, those bells rang five minutes after the others (and still do today). If they hurried, they could make

... and when the rabbit tried

it to Tom Tower in time to hear the enormous bell ring. Tom hung in the tower that had been designed by the famous architect Christopher Wren in the 1600s. (You can see the tower on page 49.)

Down below, the bell ringer began pulling on a heavy rope. A boy made a chalk mark on a blackboard for every ring. Was it that hard to keep track?

Yes, at Christ Church it was, because at nine o'clock (well, five after nine) Tom always rang 101 times. The girls knew that long ago there had been a hundred teachers. Students had to be in by nine o'clock, when the gates were locked, and the chimes reminded them of their teachers. So why does Tom ring 101 times? Because an extra teacher came in 1663, making it 101.

When the bell had rung 101 times, they borrowed a lantern and climbed the narrow, winding staircase. Round and round. Alice got slightly dizzy. At the top of the stairs was Tom, weighing more than seven tons. But Alice

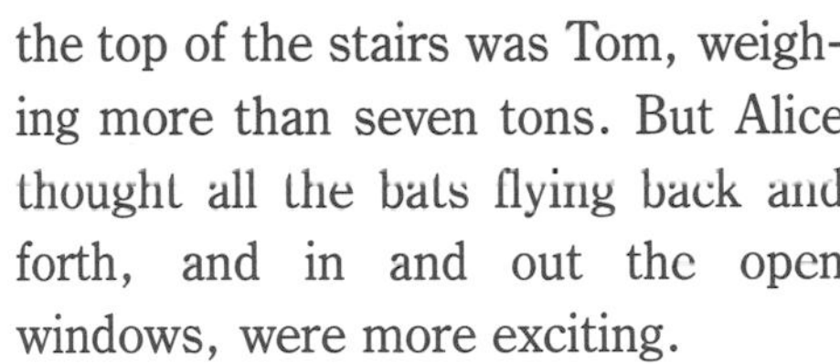

thought all the bats flying back and forth, and in and out the open windows, were more exciting.

"Let's pretend that Bob the Bat is here," said Alice. "You left the drawer slightly open, didn't you?"

"I always do that," said Mr. Dodgson.

"What's that up there?" asked Alice, wanting to climb up the ladder that went to the roof.

"That's probably where the bats live," said Mr. Dodgson. "But it's too high and dark and late. Think about tomorrow. And the day after!"

"Oh yes," said Alice. "The day after tomorrow!"

On the way home, Mr. Dodgson made up a song to the tune of "Twinkle, Twinkle, Little Star":

Twinkle, twinkle, little bat!
How I wonder what you're at!

The Day Before the Big Day

The next morning, Alice sat right up in bed and recited:

Long life to this tree, and may it prosper from this auspicious day! Its name shall be Albert!

Oh dear, what if I were to say, *Long tree to this life,* thought Alice.

But Alice had all day to practice, since it wasn't until the next day that the Prince of Wales would marry Princess Alexandra of Denmark. Not in Oxford, but at Windsor, although the wedding would be celebrated all over the country. The scary part was that Ina, Alice, and Edith, in honor of the big day, were each to plant an elm tree and give a speech. And lots of people would be watching. At the same time, it was fun to be given such an important task in honor of the Prince.

For, believe it or not, Alice actually knew the Prince. The Queen had decided that he would study at Christ Church, and that meant that the Queen thought that Alice's father's college was the best of all.

Dean Liddell's friend Professor Acland was the Prince's doctor, and the Prince lived with the Aclands for a while. Alice liked to visit them, because the professor had a pet monkey. (Just think, Alice knew *two* professors who had monkeys!)

Sometimes the Prince was invited for dinner at the Liddells'. Then Ina, Alice, and Edith would get to join the adults. They would sing three-part harmony and sometimes play their mandolins.

The Prince liked to tease Alice. Sometimes he dropped in without telling them ahead of time. One time he came into a room where Alice was trying on a dress for the seamstress. She dashed out, wearing just a petticoat, with pins flying everywhere, and the Prince said afterward, "Tell Alice that I saw her!"

Mr. Dodgson had also met the Prince. He had showed him one of his photo albums, and told the Prince that he could have whichever pictures he liked best. Alice was in two of the pictures that the Prince chose.

But Alice thought it was even more remarkable that she had met the Queen. Alice was eight at the time. The Queen came to visit her son, along with her husband, Albert (whose title wasn't King but Prince Consort), and their daughter Alice (whom so many little girls were named after). Queen Victoria had reigned a long time and was a headstrong woman whom everyone obeyed. Her influence on morality, propriety, and dressing was very strong. Ladies should preferably be covered up to the neck, and under no circumstances could they show their legs. The *Victorian* Age is

Professor Acland with his monkey

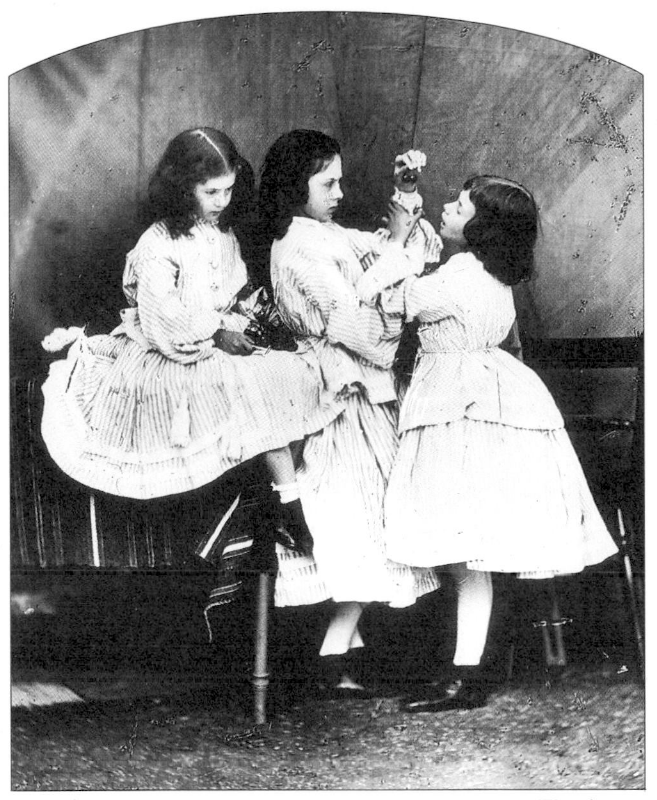

The pictures the Prince chose

named after her. When royalty came, a banquet was held in the Hall, a spacious and beautiful dining room where students and teachers ate every day. The guests of honor were seated at the High Table at the far end of the hall.

Mr. Dodgson had taken Alice down into the giant kitchen under the Hall. There she got to ride around on some big turtles. However, when Alice understood they soon would be made into soup for the royal guests, she burst into tears. It didn't matter how much she cried, the poor turtles were put into the pots anyway.

"There's something called mock-turtle soup," said Mr. Dodgson. "You don't need turtles to make it."

"Why didn't they make that, instead?" asked Alice, sobbing. "What is mock-turtle soup made from?"

"From veal," said Mr. Dodgson.

"A poor little calf!" cried Alice.

Only then she remembered how good veal cutlets taste. Oh, everything was so terrible . . .

But now she felt sorry for the Queen as well, because her husband was dead, and the Princes and Princesses had lost their father. That's why Alice named her tree Albert, in memory of the Prince Consort.

But Alice couldn't deal with sad things today. Since it was so cold out, she stayed inside and practiced her speech. And then she wrote a letter to Mr. Dodgson:

Dear Mr. Dodgson,
May I go out with you to watch the fireworks tomorrow evening?
Respectfully,

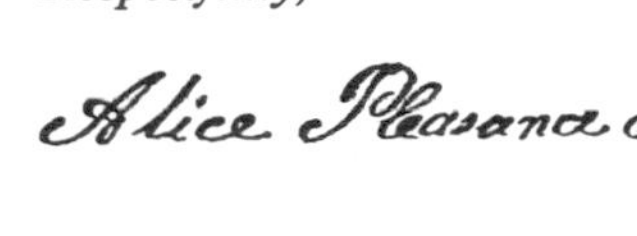

Queen Victoria

May They Be Happy!

The girls woke up early. Fortunately, it was sunny and warm. Mrs. Liddell's mother had come to see the festivities. Everyone was happy except Rhoda, who wanted to plant a tree, too.

They ate breakfast in their dressing gowns, so they wouldn't spill anything on their new dresses and petticoats, which Phoebe and Marie (their French nurse) had ironed so carefully.

The whole family (except Mrs. Liddell, who was expecting a baby in a couple of weeks) strolled over to Broad Walk, where the trees would be planted.

Mr. Dodgson was there with Edwin (his youngest brother, who was sixteen). Mr. Duckworth, the Aclands, and Professor Daubeny were there (but no monkeys). It seemed to Alice that all of Oxford was there, and her heart began beating wildly.

First Ina planted her tree, naming it Alexandra. Then it was Alice's turn:

"*Long life to this tree, and may it prosper from this auspicious day! Its name shall be Albert!*" said Alice without a stumble.

She breathed a sigh of relief. She heard Edith name her tree Victoria. People cheered and applauded. What a wedding day!

After lunch, they watched the rowing competitions. They ran into Mr. Dodgson and Edwin again. The men took the girls and Mrs. Liddell's mother to Worcester College, where more events were planned. But there were nothing there but a roasted ox. Alice thought that was dreadful. The others did, too, so they went home again.

How exciting that Alice was allowed to go out alone with Mr. Dodgson and Edwin! She held each one tightly by the hand. There were so many people out she didn't want to lose them.

There was more than just fireworks to look at. Each college had arranged an "illumination," a special show. The nicest one, Alice thought, was a high platform decorated with garlands and big fiery letters that spelled out:

MAY THEY BE HAPPY!

They stayed out for hours; Alice didn't get home until sometime after nine-thirty. It was one of the most enjoyable days she had ever known.

Mr. Dodgson thought so, too. On March 10, 1863, he wrote in his diary:

The Wedding Day of the Prince of Wales I mark with a white stone.

P.S. The elm trees named Alexandra, Albert, and Victoria lived a long time, more than a hundred years. Then they (and all the other elms on Broad Walk) got the deadly Dutch-elm disease (a contagious fungus infection). In 1977, they all had to be cut down.

MAY THEY
BE HAPPY
PRINTING
&
Stationery

Swans – Do They Exist? What about Paradoxes?

The next morning there were two notes in the Liddells' mailbox. One was for Alice: a drawing resembling yesterday's garlands. But instead of MAY THEY BE HAPPY, it said CERTAINLY NOT. It was from Mr. Dodgson. Alice saved the drawing. (Lucky the newlyweds hadn't seen it . . .)

The other note was to Alice's mother. Mr. Dodgson asked if the girls could take a long walk with him to Binsey village. Mrs. Liddell said yes, but only for Alice and Edith. And Miss Prickett.

They walked west on the path along the south riverbank. Since Mr. Dodgson was nearly deaf in his right ear, he wanted the girls to walk on his left side. Not easy, because the exciting part, the riverbank, was on his right. As usual, they had brought bread for the ducks, but today there were a couple of swans as well.

"Just think, there are swans!" said Alice.

"Whatever do you mean by that?" asked Miss Prickett.

"They look as if they would only be in fairy tales," said Alice. "Or heaven. So beautiful . . ."

"Except when they go up on land," said Edith.

"Let's pretend that the swans are enchanted princes," said Alice.

"Why not princesses?" asked Mr. Dodgson.

"The princesses, of course, are Edith and I," said Alice. "I shall give the swans some magic bread, so they'll turn back into people again."

"Good idea," said Mr. Dodgson.

"Be careful; they may bite," said Miss Prickett. "Where are your gloves?"

Alice held out a piece of bread. The closest swan hissed and snapped at both the bread and Alice's thumb. Ouch! Let go!

"What did I say?" said Miss Prickett.

"Probably the wrong kind of bread," said Mr. Dodgson, kissing Alice's thumb. "Does it hurt?"

"Stupid, rude swan," said Alice. "You may blame yourself if you stay a swan all your life!"

"But what if it *is* a swan," said Edith. "Try a duck, instead."

"The thing with ducks," said Alice, "is they are only ducks. Always."

"If they aren't enchanted swans, that is," said Mr. Dodgson.

In Binsey they visited the churchyard. Beside the church was St. Margaret's sacred well. Once upon a time there was a princess named Frideswide. An evil king wanted to marry her. Then she ran away into the forest and became a nun. One day when she was rowing on the river, she stopped at Binsey because she was thirsty. Since there was no well there, she prayed to St. Margaret and one appeared. It was not an ordinary well but a treacle well, one whose water could cure diseases. After that, everyone understood that Frideswide was a saint, and she was made the patron of Oxford. Alice knew the whole story.

"Alice, when did St. Frideswide die?" asked Miss Prickett.

"I'm not sure," said Alice.

"In the year 727," said Miss Prickett. "Write it down."

"There are at least three versions of St. Frideswide's life and death," said Mr. Dodgson.

"Which is the true one?" asked Edith.

"No one knows for sure," said Mr. Dodgson.

"What a relief I hadn't learned a wrong-truth," said Alice. "That would just take up space in my brain. Wrong-truths and impossible-truths I always try to avoid . . ."

"That was a good word," said Mr. Dodgson. "*Impossible-truth*. A new word for *paradox*."

"*Paradox*," said Alice. "That sounds like something big that has horns."

"They are big," said Mr. Dodgson, "but unusual. Shall I tell you about one?"

"Yes!" cried the girls.

"Once upon a time . . ." said Mr. Dodgson, ". . . a liar said: I always tell lies."

"Yes, and what about it?" said Alice and Edith.

"There isn't any more," said Mr. Dodgson. "That's the entire paradox. Think about it."

Alice thought a minute. Then she said, "If one says that one always tells lies, then *that* is a lie, since it's the truth. On the other hand . . . no, that wouldn't work . . ."

"You've got it, Alice. That was a bit of brain exercise. The subject is *logic*."

As they were talking, Edith leaned far down into the well. But it was too dark to see anything.

"Careful," said Miss Prickett. "You may fall in."

"Yes," said Alice. "And at the bottom is a horrible paradox that wants to eat you up!"

"Would you like to hear what really is down there?" asked Mr. Dodgson.

"Yes!" cried the girls.

"Once upon a time," he began, "there were three little girls named Elsie, Lacie, and Tillie . . ."

Ah, thought Alice. Elsie must be short for Lorina Charlotte (L.C.); Lacie is Alice with the letters switched around; and Tillie is from Matilda. (Edith was called that sometimes.)

"The three girls lived at the bottom of a treacle well," continued Mr. Dodgson.

What happened to the girls and how the story ended, no one is left who remembers. It was just one of those little stories that buzzes off and is forgotten like a summer midge.

And so it was time for tea. Luckily, Miss Prickett had relatives living in Binsey, so they were invited for tea and jam sandwiches. Then they walked all the long way home. Most likely, Mr. Dodgson told a new and exciting story for them as they walked on his left side.

But the ducks were still ducks. And the swans were only swans.

"That's the way it goes when one has the wrong kind of bread," said Mr. Dodgson.

Sent Off to Grandmother's

In the beginning of April, Ina, Alice, and Edith were sent to the Dean's mother's house, along with Miss Prickett. Their mother was going to have a baby and needed peace and quiet at home.

There was peace and quiet at Grandmother's home, Hetton Lawn, near Cheltenham — too much peace and quiet, thought Alice. Charlotte and Amelia, her maiden aunts, who lived there, were not much use as playmates. Nor were her grandparents.

"If only Mr. Dodgson were here," said Alice.

"We'll invite him!" said Ina, going to ask Grandmother.

And Grandmother said yes! Ina wrote right away, inviting him to come for lunch.

Of course Mr. Dodgson accepted. He took a train to Cheltenham on Saturday morning. Alice and Miss Prickett met him at the station.

"I have a new baby brother!" shouted Alice. "And the Prince of Wales has promised to be his godfather. And he has decided his name shall be Albert Edward Arthur. Imagine how good it must be to have a prince for one's godfather . . ."

"I know. I know," said Mr. Dodgson.

What he also knew was that the new baby was tiny and weak and sickly. But he didn't say anything to Alice about it. Instead, he told a story while they walked the one and a half miles to Hetton Lawn. It was about a rabbit, but no one remembers it any longer. They arrived in time for lunch. After they had eaten, everyone took a horse-drawn carriage to Birdlip to admire the view. They asked if they could walk all the way home, through the hills, with Mr. Dodgson. And Miss Prickett.

Mr. Dodgson stayed for dinner. Then, since the last train had gone, he checked into a hotel.

The following day, it was pouring. The girls convinced Mr. Dodgson to stay on.

"Otherwise, we will die of boredom," said Alice.

The picture that Grandmother chose

"We will shrink from tedium," said Ina.

"Then I could put you in a little box," said Mr. Dodgson, "and take you out when *I* was bored."

Mr. Dodgson spent all day with the girls and Miss Prickett in the classroom at Grandmother's. They looked at Mr. Dodgson's photo album, and Grandmother was allowed to pick out a picture. She chose one of Alice wearing a wreath of flowers.

They had lessons, too — mathematics, for example. Mr. Dodgson taught them to count with little cakes instead of numbers. He said that cake problems were every bit as good for you as number problems.

And when it was time for writing, Mr. Dodgson suggested they make their own magazine.

"Can we do that ourselves?" asked Edith.

"It's ever so easy," said Mr. Dodgson. "I made lots of them when I was a child."

"Such as?" asked Alice.

"*The Comet,* for example. And *Rosebud* and *The Rectory Umbrella* and *Mischmasch.*" (*Mischmasch* is the German spelling of "mishmash.")

"*Mischmasch*?" said Alice. "What's that?"

"A mixture of this, that, and the other thing, whatever, and some nonsense," he said. "Plus some poems and mazes and riddles."

"Why didn't you bring them?" asked Alice.

"They're at Croft," he said. "But I can bring a few to Oxford if you'd like. Make your own in the meantime. *The Hetton Times . . .*"

VERY SWEET LITTLE BROTHER BORN, Alice wrote for her headline. *An unusually handsome baby boy was born the day before yesterday to Dean and Mrs. H. G. Liddell of Christ Church.*

"How do you know he is sweet?" asked Edith. "We haven't even seen him yet."

"Mama always has sweet children," said Alice.

"You shouldn't flatter yourself," said Ina.

"Oh dear," said Alice, embarrassed. "I was only thinking of you and Edith and Rhoda."

They didn't have time to finish the magazine, because dinner was served early. They were going to Cheltenham to see Herr Döbler's Enchanted Palace of Illusions. Herr Döbler was a famous magician from Vienna. It was most likely Mr. Dodgson's idea.

Cakes in a row

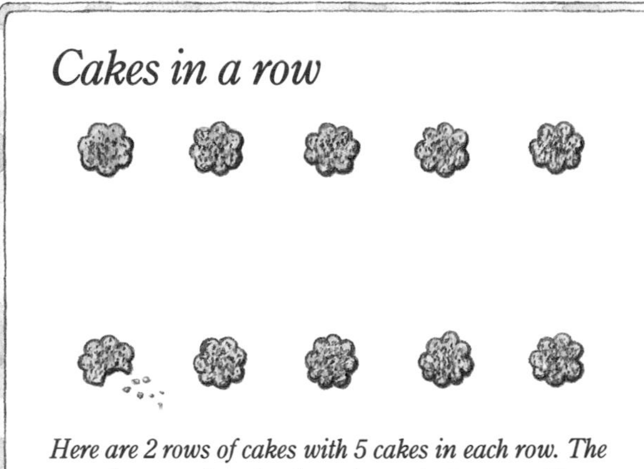

Here are 2 rows of cakes with 5 cakes in each row. The space between the cakes in each row is the same. Now move 4 cakes so that you'll have 5 rows with 4 cakes in each row. (Hint: Each cake can be in more than one row at the same time . . .) The solution? Turn the page!

Grandmother's Big Looking-Glass

"It's a pity you can't do magic tricks," Alice told Mr. Dodgson the next day. "Can't I?" he asked. "See your grandmother's big looking-glass over the mantel. I made a little girl disappear into just such a looking-glass."

"How?" asked Edith. "But don't show me."

"It's a secret," he said. "But she went right through the looking-glass, to the other side."

"Did she stay there forever?" asked Alice.

"No, she came out again," said Mr. Dodgson. "And although it had only been a second, quite a lot happened to her behind the looking-glass."

And he told them about the land through the looking-glass, where everything was *reversed.* Time, for example, went *backwards.* Like this: First you bandaged your knee, then you said "Ouch," and finally you hurt yourself.

"If time went backwards here," said Ina, "we would just get younger and younger."

"That would be nice," said Mr. Dodgson. "Within certain limits, of course."

"I'm surprised you haven't invented a time machine," said Alice, "so you could stop when everything was as good as it could be."

"But I have," said Mr. Dodgson.

"You have?" said Alice. "Really?"

"It's my camera," said Mr. Dodgson. "When I took that picture of you with a wreath of flowers, I stopped time. You are seven years old forever."

"I understand what you mean," said Alice. "But that's only a picture. Not a real Alice."

She pulled up a chair, climbed on it, and looked at herself in the mirror.

"Is this the real Alice?" she asked.

"It depends on what you mean by *real,*" said Mr. Dodgson.

"Real means real, of course," said Alice.

"Don't be so sure," said Mr. Dodgson.

"Be careful, Alice!" cried Edith, running up and pulling Alice's skirt. "What if you disappeared into the looking-glass . . ."

Sometimes Edith thought it was hard to know the difference between *real* and *make-believe* when Mr. Dodgson was around. But he would never make Alice disappear. And not Ina. And not herself, either. Possibly Miss Prickett . . .

The next day Mr. Dodgson left his hotel and went over to pick up the girls and Miss Prickett. They walked to Cheltenham, where he left them at the riding school. Then he took the train home to Croft. Easter vacation had started, and he mustn't forget to look for *Mischmasch* ...

Cakes in a row

The solution to the cake problem on page 61

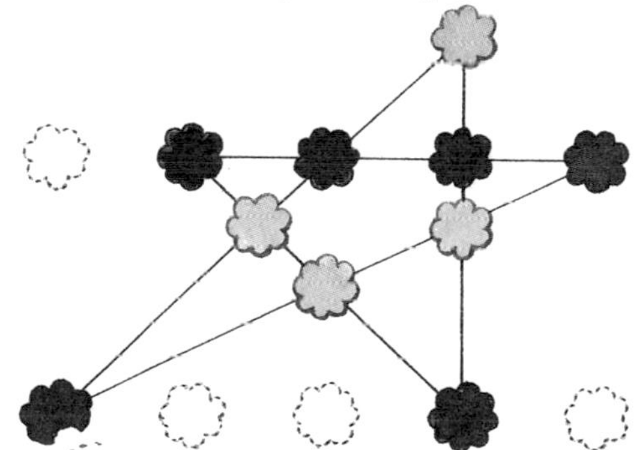

More cakes in a row

1. *Put 9 cakes in 8 rows with 3 cakes in every row.*

2. *Put 9 cakes in 9 rows with 3 cakes in every row.*

Solutions on page 89.

You can make up some new problems of your own, but you'll have to use coins or buttons instead of cakes, if you ate them.

Mischmasch

he first day everybody was back in Oxford, Harry asked Mr. Dodgson if he'd like to go boating. It turned out to be an enjoyable day with Harry, Ina, Alice, Edith, and Miss Prickett.

A few days later, Alice twisted her foot and wasn't allowed to go out. She immediately sent for Mr. Dodgson to keep her and Rhoda company. He arrived with a box under his arm.

"Did you bring *Mischmasch*?" asked Alice.

"Of course," he said, opening the box. "And I brought along *The Rectory Umbrella* as well."

The girls admired the cover. It showed a man with an open umbrella; JOKES, RIDDLES, FUN, POETRY, AND TALES were written on it. Flying overhead were little men who were dropping stones labeled WOE, GLOOM, ENNUI and other unpleasant things. Down below were fairies carrying baskets filled with GOOD HUMOUR, TASTE, LIVELINESS, KNOWLEDGE, MIRTH.

"That's the sort of umbrella I need," said Alice. "For *worry*. I'm worried about my baby brother."

"What if he dies and becomes an angel?" said Rhoda. "Just like our brother Arthur."

"We must pray to God that he may be well soon," said Mr. Dodgson.

"What is *that*?" said Rhoda, seeing a drawing of a hippopotamus in *Mischmasch*.

"I call it 'Innocence,'" said Mr. Dodgson. "Its inspiration is a picture by Joshua Reynolds."

Alice found a maze in *Mischmasch*.

"If you lay tissue paper over it, you won't need to draw on the magazine," Mr. Dodgson said. "I recall a giant maze I once made at Croft."

"Do you still have it?" asked Rhoda.

"No," said Mr. Dodgson. "It was one I made stamping down the snow in the front garden."

"I hope we shall have snow this winter," said Rhoda.

"Would you like to hear a *Mischmasch* poem?" asked Mr. Dodgson.

Twas bryllyg, and ye slythy toves
Did gyre and gymble in ye wabe:
All mimsy were ye borogoves;
And ye mome raths outgrabe.

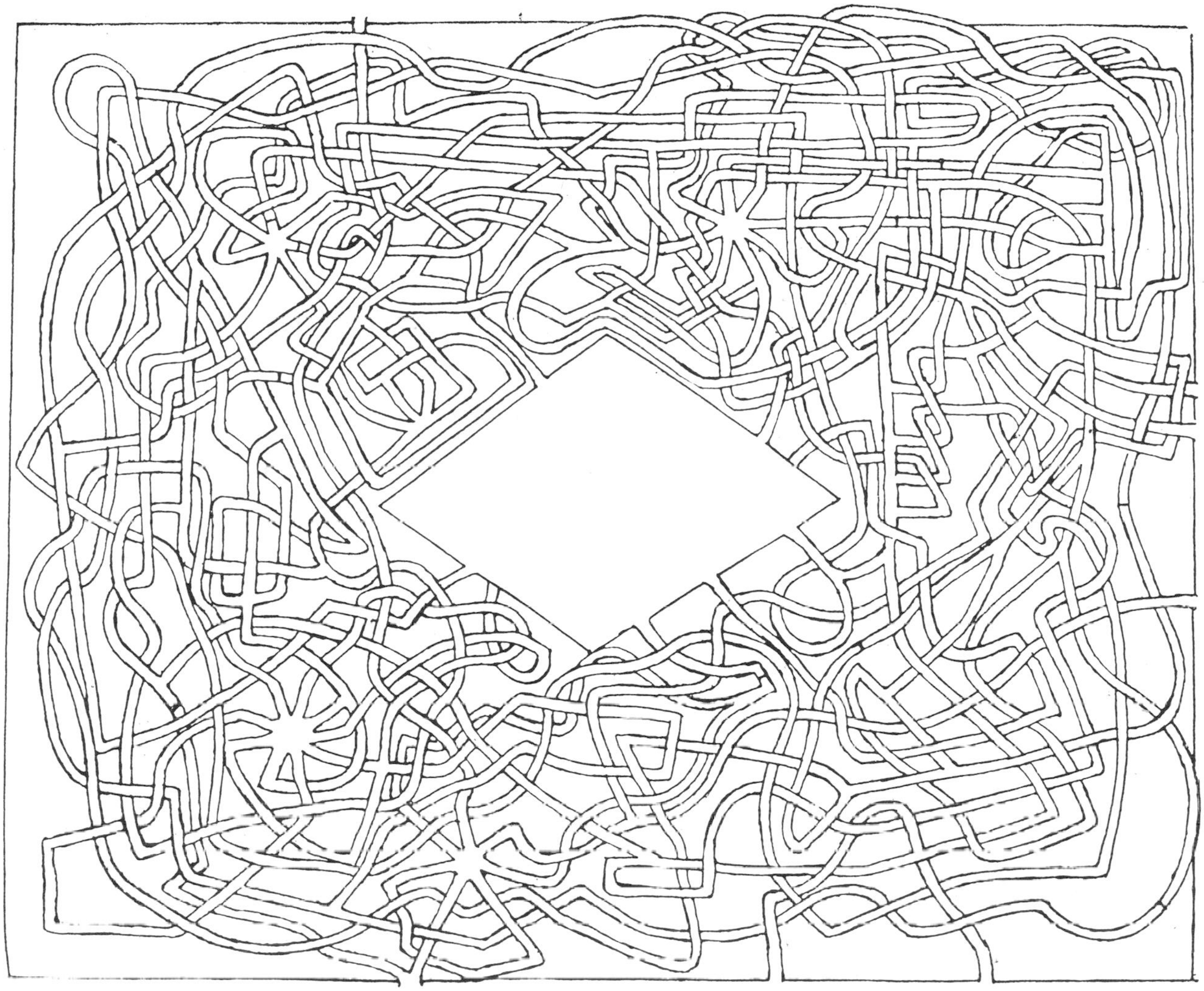

The object is to start from the open space in the middle and get yourself out of the maze. You are allowed *to go over and under paths that cross each other, but* you are forbidden *to continue on one if there is a line across the path.*

"What is a 'tove'?" Alice asked.

"It's difficult to know," said Mr. Dodgson.

"But you have written it yourself," said Alice.

"Perhaps it's a cross between a lizard and a badger, a bit like a corkscrew. But I must go now. This drawing fits very well, because *finis* means 'end' in Latin. I shall see you tomorrow."

The fourth of May was Alice's birthday; she was eleven years old. She got a nice book from Mr. Dodgson, but not the one she really wanted. It wasn't ready yet. Mr. Dodgson was still drawing. What in the world does a gryphon look like?

But in spite of many good times, it was a sad spring. On May 28, Alice's baby brother died. The girls were overwhelmed by grief.

It didn't even help to have a prince for a godfather, thought Alice, before she fell asleep that night. At least the baby has a brother up there in heaven.

The Deer That Whispered

One day Mr. Dodgson took a walk to the Grove, the deer park at Magdalen College. Alice, Edith, and Rhoda got to go with him. And Miss Prickett. The deer were rather shy; they absolutely did not want to be petted. But they came closer when Alice held out a handful of grass.

One deer came really close. It stretched its head over the fence, nuzzled Alice, and blew in her ear. Then it quickly grabbed the grass she was holding, but carefully, without biting as the swan had done.

"Oh, how frightened I was!" said Alice.

"It looked as if it was whispering something to you," said Edith.

"Just don't say what," said Mr. Dodgson. "Deer secrets must be kept to yourself."

"I'll never tell," Alice told the deer. "Now let's pretend it becomes tame and follows us home."

"It could live in the garden," said Edith.

"But perhaps it would want to see other deer," said Alice. "Perhaps it would get bored."

"Then we shall take two," said Rhoda.

"What would your mother say?" said Miss Prickett.

"But we're only pretending," said Alice.

"Are we?" asked Rhoda.

Professor Buckland with one of his monkeys

"I really hope so," said Miss Prickett, "If you were to decide, you would like to live like Professor Buckland."

Professor Buckland had lived at Christ Church before the Liddells arrived He was a professor of geology (the study of rocks). He had a bear lumbering around the house, guinea pigs running around on the floor, and monkeys climbing up the curtains. Mr. Ruskin (Alice's future art teacher) told how he had once been invited to Professor Buckland's for a dinner of grilled crocodile and mice in batter. Then he had to fight with the monkeys for dessert (which was fruit).

"Now the deer is gone," said Edith.

"Clearly, he wasn't interested in moving in with you just today," said Mr. Dodgson. "Alice, make a sketch of a *gargoyle** instead; they almost always hold still."

"*Almost* always?" said Alice.

"We shall see," said Mr. Dodgson. Alice chose a garoyle on the wall by Magdalen College, one with a big smile because a little man is holding up the corners of its mouth. After she'd drawn it, she said, "May we go into Magdalen's quad?"

"Goodness, no," said Miss Prickett. "It's useless to sketch such pagan monsters."

"But compared to them, angels and madonnas become even more beautiful," said Alice.

Mr. Dodgson agreed, and they went in.

"Look at this one carrying its young on its back," said Alice. "What kind of animal is that?"

"I believe it's a hippopotamus," said Mr. Dodgson.

Rhoda had to use binoculars to see the statues, because they were high up on the stone pedestals around the open quad.

"*Your* hippopotamus was better," Rhoda told Mr. Dodgson. "Why does that other one have a face on its stomach?"

"To discourage gluttony," said Miss Prickett.

"That's one of the Deadly Sins," said Alice. "It means to overeat. See how much we are learning here, Miss Prickett."

So they started home, first along the High and then along Merton Street. In front of Merton College gate, Alice borrowed the binoculars.

"A unicorn! What if there were unicorns in the deer park . . ."

"There aren't any unicorns," said Miss Prickett.

"Except in stories," said Edith.

"Let's pretend that there are," said Alice, "and that we meet one out on the Meadow . . ."

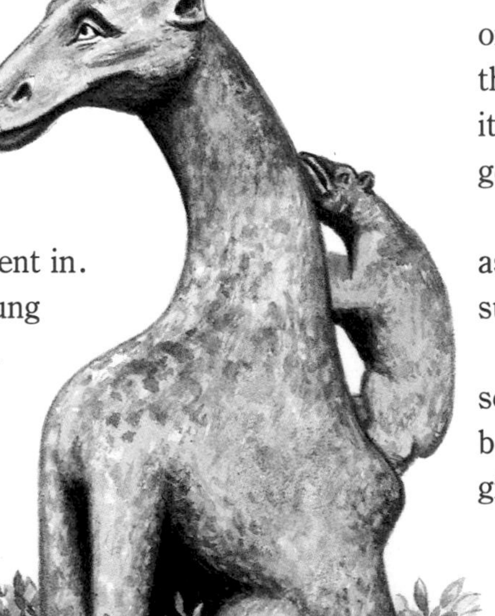

"Then you must sit down at once," said Mr. Dodgson, "so the unicorn may come and put its head in your lap, and be gentle as a lamb."

"How do you know that?" asked Rhoda. "Can you be sure?"

"Absolutely," said Mr. Dodgson. "A unicorn likes nothing better than to rest its head in a girl's lap."

"To the far right you see John the Baptist," said Miss Prickett. "And next to him is Walter de Merton, who founded Merton College in 1264. And in the center you see the book in Revelation with its seven seals, guarded by the Lion and the Lamb."

". . . and the Unicorn," said Edith.

"But look down at the bottom!" said Alice.

Down on the ground, beneath the statues, rabbits were running all around in little holes.

"They look almost real," said Alice. "Are they the ones you meant that sometimes move?"

"Who can say?" said Mr. Dodgson. "But I was thinking of some other ones. We can go see them tomorrow."

* *Watch Out for GARGOYLES!*

"Gargoyle" is connected to the French word gargouille, which means the gurgle of water in a roof drain. Rainspouts were decorated with small sculptures which spilled the water out and kept it from running down the side of a building.

In England, especially Oxford, architects and carvers adopted the French custom, placing little men, dragons, and devils wherever they could under the roof.

They were usually carved in limestone; Oxford has always had its talented stonecutters, such as the O'Shea brothers, who carved the monkeys, cats, and other animals around the windows at the University Museum.

Alice knew them well, because there had been a big fight about them. In the end they were allowed to stay there, and they are still there today.

It's a good idea to watch out in Oxford; many of the gargoyles are ... well, not exactly angels.

Royalty Is Coming!

That night Alice dreamed that she met a real unicorn. She was sitting in a meadow, or perhaps it was in a tapestry, for there were so many flowers and little rabbits all around. And the unicorn rested its head in her lap. But then Miss Prickett came — and Alice woke up.

There wasn't time for more gargoyles, because the girls had to try on their new dresses. The royal newlyweds were paying a visit to Oxford — and staying with the Liddells!

Mrs. Liddell had a lot to do. She furnished a new bedroom for the royal couple. On the table was an album with Mr. Dodgson's photographs.

Ina also asked Mr. Dodgson to help them get their booth ready for the charity bazaar.

The next day the royal couple opened the bazaar. The girls sold kittens. Alice begged Mr. Dodgson to ask the Princess to buy hers (she didn't dare ask herself), but the Princess had just bought Ina's kitten.

Lots of people came, wanting to buy things. No one remembered Rhoda. Where was she?

Mr. Dodgson and Edith went searching for her. So many people were there that it was like looking for a needle in a haystack. At last they found her, calmly "helping out" at another booth, not far away.

Mr. Dodgson picked Rhoda up, and then, guiding Edith through the crowd, he brought her back to the Liddells' booth.

The next day, at Christ Church, the Prince was to receive an honorary degree from Oxford University. The girls stood with the royal guests under a big canopy. They were dressed in their finest clothes. But Mr. Dodgson watched it all from a high window, through his tclcscopc.

In between festivities there was even time for a little croquet with the royal guests. Mr. Dodgson asked to photograph the Prince.

"Thank you, but no," said the Prince. "I am so terribly tired of being photographed."

Mr. Dodgson had to content himself with a picture of the royal bedroom (after they had left). He had Alice and Ina sit by the window, so it was a good picture, anyway. That evening he went to the circus with the girls and Miss Prickett.

Mr. Dodgson felt almost like a member of the family when, a few days later, he was asked to organize a boat trip for Dean and Mrs. Liddell, Grandfather Liddell, Ina, Alice, Edith, and Rhoda, plus a few guests. He rented a large boat with four pairs of oars, so there would be room for everyone.

It was a nice trip to Nuneham. A horse and carriage was waiting there, but there wasn't room for Ina, Alice, Edith, and Mr. Dodgson; they had to take the train home from Abingdon. What fun!

That day was truly worth a white stone!

Something Has Happened

Suddenly it was summer, and the Liddells left for Llandudno, as usual. Mrs. Liddell didn't let the girls say goodbye to Mr. Dodgson, and before they left she took the old cigar box where they kept all their letters from him.

"One can't keep all this rubbish," she said.

Mrs. Liddell was so firm that the old letters ended up in the fire. Was she angry with Mr. Dodgson again? Oh well, it would probably sort itself out by autumn.

Alice's father decided to hire an artist, Mr. Richmond, to paint a portrait of Ina, Alice, and Edith. For seven whole weeks he lived with the Liddells, and the girls had to pose for him every day. Oh, how dull! And they never got as much as a peek at the painting before it was finished.

"Just think, Mr. Dodgson needs only forty-two seconds to take a picture of us," said Alice. "How could we ever have complained about that?"

It took seven weeks to paint ...

... but only forty-two seconds to photograph

In the autumn, Mr. Dodgson stayed away from the Liddells. (We don't know why, but a page has been torn out of his diary, the day following the boat trip he had enjoyed so much. So no one would notice, the text was changed a little on the next page — but not in Mr. Dodgson's handwriting.)

Alice must have thought it was sad not to see her friend Mr. Dodgson. But she had a lot to do that autumn. Since she had grown during the summer, the seamstress had to come and make her some new dresses. Alice's hair had also gotten longer, and sometimes she talked Phoebe into curling it with the curling iron (Alice thought short, straight hair looked a bit childish). And then there were dance lessons, both classical ballet and social dancing, and lots of parties.

Wilfred's gryphon

But, in spite of everything, just before Christmas Mr. Dodgson was invited to the Liddells' to play croquet. Croquet in December? No, it was too cold; instead, he had tea with the girls in the nursery. Mrs. Liddell stayed out of sight, but then she was going to have a new baby soon.

"The story that you promised me," said Alice, "I may give up on it."

"No," said Mr. Dodgson. "A promise is a promise."

He went home and worked on the illustrations for the story. (His brother Wilfred helped him with the gryphon.) Then he gave the day a white stone in his diary.

Spring came. On March 10, Alice got a healthy, spirited little sister, whom they named Violet. On May 4, Alice turned twelve, but she didn't get her story. Mr. Dodgson didn't even come by to wish her a happy birthday; he was in London attending the theater.

Little Violet

It was some time before Mr. Dodgson finished the illustrations. Some friends of his, the MacDonalds, read the story.

"I wish there were sixty thousand volumes of it," said little Greville MacDonald.

Mr. Dodgson with Mrs. MacDonald and her children: Greville, Mary, Irene, and Grace, 1863

"You *must* publish this story," said Mrs. MacDonald. "It's really quite amazing!"

Mary Hilton Badcock

Mr. Dodgson was so happy that he went to a printer and asked him to set and print page proofs. But were his own drawings good enough? He asked different people for advice, and understood at last that he must have a real illustrator, who would have to do everything over.

He asked John Tenniel, who was an illustrator for the well-known humor magazine *Punch.* After a lot of persuasion, Mr. Tenniel agreed to illustrate the book. Mr. Dodgson sent him a picture of a little girl named Mary Hilton Badcock.

"Use her as a model," suggested Mr. Dodgson.

"I no more need one than you should need a multiplication table to work a mathematical problem!" answered Mr. Tenniel.

The handwritten story was called *Alice's Adventures Underground,* but the published book would be called *Alice's Adventures in Wonderland.* The author would not be called Charles Lutwidge Dodgson but a name he had made up: Lewis Carroll. He used his real name only when he wrote mathematics books. It wasn't a good idea to use your real name in silly storybooks.

He added some more chapters and changed a little here and there. Then he decided that Mr. Tenniel should make exactly forty-two illustrations and showed him his own.

John Tenniel

Alice Gets Too Big – Almost

One day Mr. Dodgson met Alice and Rhoda with Miss Prickett on the Broad.

"I promised to tell you about gargoyles that can move, some time ago," Mr. Dodgson said.

"Oh yes," said Alice. "I had quite forgotten."

"I was thinking about these," he said.

Mr. Dodgson pointed up at a row of bearded old men standing in a half circle around the Sheldonian Theatre (where Oxford University's graduation ceremonies are held). They looked like Roman emperors; wind and bad weather had worn down their noses and other facial features.

"They've become tired of standing guard here," said Mr. Dodgson, "so sometimes . . ."

"So sometimes what?" said Rhoda excitedly.

"They simply climb down," he said.

"Can one believe such a thing?" said Alice.

"If one wants to," said Mr. Dodgson. "But they do wait until it's quite late. Then they go over there to the tavern. So they say."

Oh, he's always making things up, thought Alice, but she went with him up to the cupola of the Sheldonian anyway and looked at the view. Then they went to the printer to see the page proofs. Mr. Dodgson wasn't at all satisfied and asked the printer to do it again.

The printer looked worried, and Rhoda said, "What a fine hat Mr. Printer has!"

It was made from a folded printed sheet. Mr. Dodgson asked the printer if he could make one like it for Rhoda. She got to take it home, so she would remember how to fold it. Alice didn't want a paper hat.

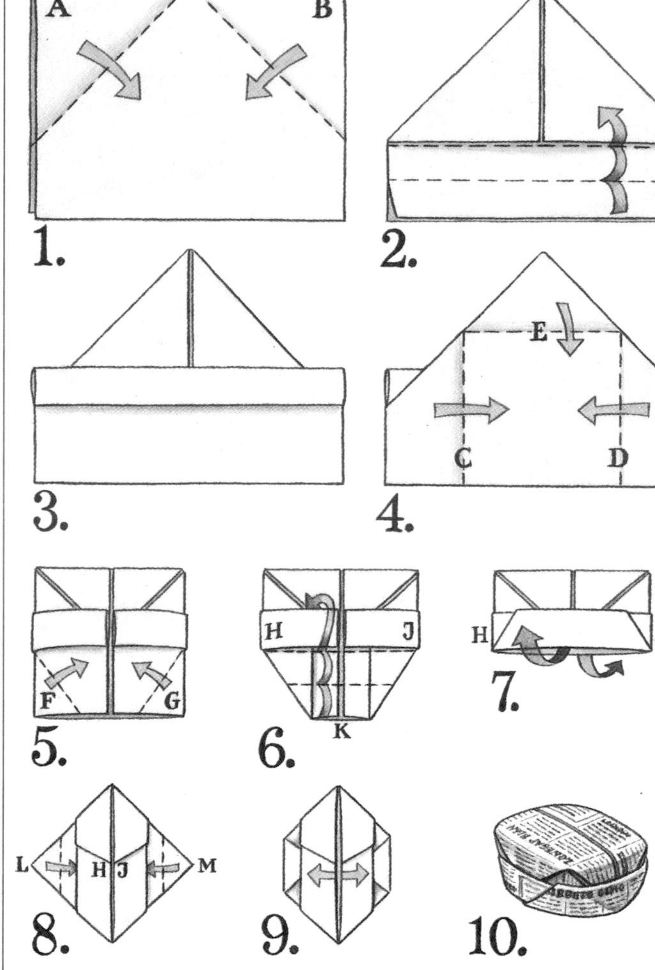

Here's How You Fold a Hat

1. *Fold a newspaper page in two (fold on top) and turn down corners A and B.*
2. *Fold the top layer of the bottom edge up one turn …*
3. *… and then another.*
4. *Turn it over. Fold over the sides at C and D. Fold down the top at E.*
5. *Fold up the bottom corners F and G.*
6. *Fold up K twice and tuck it behind H and J.*
7. *Put your thumbs inside the hat and pull it out until H and J meet …*
8. *… like this. Tuck in L and M so that …*
9. *… the points are tucked under H and J. Open up the hat and put it on!*
10. *A bigger piece of paper makes a bigger hat, of course.*

36

than she expected: before she had drunk half the bottle, she found her head pressing against the ceiling, and she stooped to save her neck from being broken, and hastily put down the bottle, saying to herself "that's quite enough — I hope I shan't grow any more — I wish I hadn't drunk so much!"

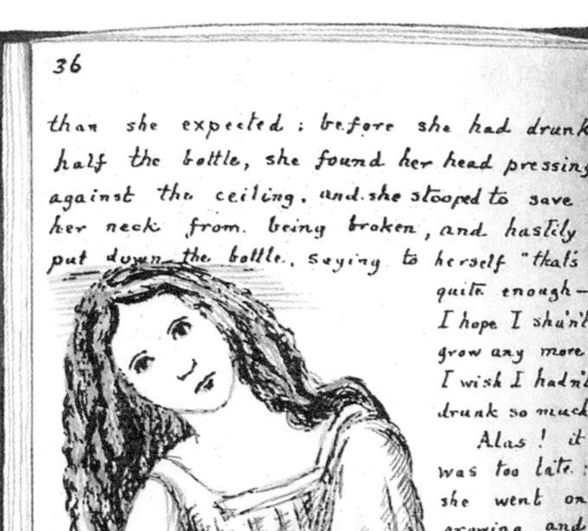

Alas! it was too late: she went on growing and growing, and very soon had to kneel down: in another minute there was not room even for this, and she tried the effect of lying down, with one elbow against the door, and the other arm curled round her head. Still she went on growing, and as a last resource she put one arm out of the window, and one foot up the chimney, and said to herself "now I can do no more — what *will* become of me?"

37.

Mr. Dodgson got the feeling that now he *must* finish the story — before Alice outgrew it. He had planned to give it to her when the published book came out, but now he didn't dare wait that long. Not even until Christmas. So Alice got the book as an early Christmas present on November 26, 1864. Finally!

Alice was delighted. She read the story over and over again. It was displayed on the table in the sitting room, so everyone could see it.

I shall keep this book all my life, thought Alice.

And here ends the story of the friendship between Alice Liddell and Mr. Dodgson.

P.S. What later happened to them (and to the books) you can read about in the rest of *this* book.

Alice recognized a lot of things in the book's pictures. The tree looked like the big chestnut in her own garden. And the Cheshire Cat acted just like Dinah ...

The Hatter looks a lot like Mr. Carter, the furniture dealer on the High ...

What Happened Afterward

● The Liddell girls and Mr. Dodgson rarely met, unless they happened to see each other at Christ Church or in town somewhere.

Harry, Ina, and Alice had gotten too heavy for the old pony, Tommy. He was allowed to retire to the stable, and Dean Liddell bought a new pony.

One day, when Alice was out riding with her father, her horse stumbled and fell. Alice landed so hard that she broke her thighbone.

She had to stay home to rest her leg for six weeks. During all that time, Mr. Dodgson never once came to visit her (but he wasn't invited, either).

On May 4, 1865, Alice turned thirteen. The eleventh of May, Mr. Dodgson wrote in his diary:

Met Alice and Miss Prickett in the quadrangle: Alice seems changed a good deal, and hardly for the better — probably going through the usual awkward stage of transition.

Alice meets the Dodo (Do-do-dodgson). Behind him the Duck (Duckworth) and one of Professor Daubeny's monkeys ...

The Book Finished

● Mr. Dodgson himself paid both Mr. Tenniel for his pictures and Mr. Macmillan for printing the book. But then he insisted the book be *perfect.* He told Mr. Tenniel how every picture should look. And Mr. Macmillan had to run proofs.

Finally the book was ready to be printed (with two thousand copies in the first printing). Mr. Dodgson decided that the books should be covered in red cloth, except Alice's own copy; that one he had bound in white vellum (parchment).

Alice got the printed book on July 4, 1865, exactly three years from the day she had first heard the story.

Now it was Mr. Tenniel who was fussy. When he said the pictures had been badly printed, Mr. Dodgson had everything done again. Even Alice had to return her copy. (But the cover was removed and used for the new book.)

Alice and her sisters fell in love with the book. Other children did, too. In those days, there were nowhere near as many children's books as today; the ones that did exist were moralistic, created mainly to keep children in line.

Mr. Dodgson's book was made for children to *enjoy.* His stories were so imaginative and full of surprises, and grownups didn't always know best (it was actually Alice who did). Girls who read the book must have especially liked the main character, since she was a determined *girl;* that was *very* unusual.

The Gryphon and the sad Mock Turtle that Alice had cried over earlier ...

... and Famous

● Some newspapers said the book was the worst sort of rubbish and it posed a danger for children. But many others thought it was an unusually good book.

Word of the unusual children's book spread throughout England. Mr. Macmillan had to print more books, and Mr. Dodgson finally earned back the money he had paid out — and then some more.

The book became known even outside of England. In 1869 it came out in Germany and France. (But Mr. Dodgson wasn't happy that Bill, the lizard who gets kicked through the chimney, was called Jacques in France.)

Alice in America

● *Alice's Adventures in Wonderland* was published in the United States in 1866 by Appletons in New York. *The Nation* reviewed the book on December 13, 1866, saying: "This is one of the best children's books we ever met with . . . The illustrations are also excellent, for Mr. Tenniel always excels in such things."

Mr. Dodgson also wrote a poem about how the story came to be. He meant for it to come before the story itself, but not all editions of the book include it there. Here it is:

All in the golden afternoon
 Full leisurely we glide;
For both our oars, with little skill,
 By little arms are plied,
While little hands make vain pretence
 Our wanderings to guide.

Ah, cruel Three! In such an hour
 Beneath such dreamy weather,
To beg a tale of breath too weak
 To stir the tiniest feather!
Yet what can one poor voice avail
 Against three tongues together?

Imperious Prima flashes forth
 Her edict "to begin it" —
In gentler tone Secunda hopes
 "There will be nonsense in it!" —
While Tertia interrupts the tale
 Not *more* than once a minute.

Anon, to sudden silence won,
 In fancy they pursue
The dream-child moving through a land
 Of wonders wild and new,
In friendly chat with bird or beast —
 And half believe it true.

And ever, as the story drained
 The wells of fancy dry,
And faintly strove that weary one
 To put the subject by,
"The rest next time —" "It *is* next time!"
 The happy voices cry.

Thus grew the tale of Wonderland:
 Thus slowly, one by one,
Its quaint events were hammered out —
 And now the tale is done,
And home we steer, a merry crew.
 Beneath the setting sun.

Alice! a childish story take,
 And with a gentle hand
Lay it where Childhood's dreams are twined
 In Memory's mystic band,
Like pilgrim's wither'd wreath of flowers
 Pluck'd in a far-off land.

Rabbits pop up here and there, both in Alice's life and in the story ...

Growing or shrinking with cakes didn't work in real life, but it did in the story ...

The Carpenter's hat is folded just like the one on page 74!

The White Queen looks like Phoebe; the Red Queen, like Miss Prickett!

Through the Looking-Glass

● Because of the book, Mr. Dodgson (or, more correctly, Lewis Carroll) became a famous person. He got fan mail, and people asked for his autograph, but he refused to sign autographs. Any letter addressed to "Lewis Carroll" he returned, after writing ADDRESSEE UNKNOWN on it.

Encouraged by his success, Mr. Dodgson decided to write another Alice book. He called it *Through the Looking-Glass, and What Alice Found There.* In that book Alice steps right through a mirror (suspiciously like the one at her grandmother's), and into the astonishing Looking-Glass world.

Everything behind the mirror was reversed, and time went backwards. The book is like a chess game; each chapter stands for a move. The strange poem from *Mischmasch* is there, too; Mr. Dodgson called it "Jabberwocky."

He asked Mr. Tenniel to illustrate the book, but Mr. Tenniel firmly refused. It had been too hard the first time. However, Mr. Dodgson was a stubborn man, and he finally succeeded in talking Mr. Tenniel into doing it.

Alice looks a little older in *Through the Looking-Glass.* She has a fancier pinafore and striped stockings (high style at the time). And she is wearing a headband, which ever since has been called an Alice band in England.

Mr. Dodgson was very pleased with the drawing of the monstrous Jabberwock. But was it too monstrous? He asked about thirty mothers he knew for their opinion. No, they said, their children hadn't been frightened (lucky for them!), so the Jabberwock got to stay.

In one chapter Alice meets a "wasp in a wig." Mr. Tenniel wrote to Mr. Dodgson:

Don't think me brutal, but I am bound to say that the "wasp" chapter doesn't

Many artists have drawn Alice playing croquet. From left: Mr. Dodgson himself, John Tenniel, Arthur Rackham, Robert Högfeldt

The real Alice couldn't make friends with a deer, but in the story she did!

Jabberwock

Alice's Unicorn appears in the story. The Lion seems nicer than those on the staircase

interest me in the least, & I can't see my way to a picture. If you want to shorten the book, I can't help thinking — with all submission — that there is your opportunity.

Mr. Dodgson agreed to get rid of the wasp-in-a-wig.

In December 1871, Lorina, Alice, and Edith each got a copy of the new book. By then Alice was nineteen years old.

Alice in 125 Languages

● The new book became at least as famous as the first one. In England today, both grownups and children can recite "Jabberwocky." Only the Bible and Shakespeare's works are more quoted than the Alice books.

Both books have been widely translated. Before the 125th anniversary of the first book's publication someone in Australia collected Alice in 125 different languages. (Compare that to *Winnie-the-Pooh,* translated into some thirty-one languages, or *Pippi Longstocking,* into fifty-eight.)

What Did He Mean?

● Psychoanalysts and other educated people have racked their brains, trying to explain the stories. What did Lewis Carroll really *mean*? What did he *really* mean? Did he know *himself* what he meant? If anyone asked him, he would have said that he only meant to tell an amusing story to three little girls.

There are many adult books about Lewis Carroll/Charles Dodgson and his work. If you're interested, you can find some of them listed on page 92. Except for what has already been said, this book doesn't try to explain the Alice books. Instead, we'll tell you about Mr. Dodgson's other child-friends (after Alice).

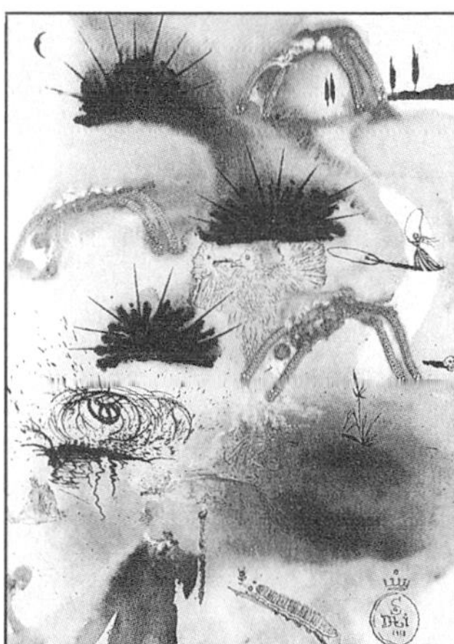

Tove Jansson, Franz Haacken, Nicole Claveloux, and Salvador Dali

Mr. Dodgson's New Child-Friends

● When Alice had grown too big, Mr. Dodgson found new child-friends. Often they were the children of other teachers and professors at Oxford. When he visited them, he spent most of his time in the nursery. If the parents came in, they might find him under a table.

"We're playing lions," the children would say.

Or he might be telling a story or drawing or playing a game.

Xie (pronounced *Eksi*) Kitchin became one of his best child-friends. He often took pictures of her. The Hatch sisters were other favorites.

He also became acquainted with children riding on trains. He always traveled with a black Gladstone bag, full of games and toys, that he took out if there was a child in the same compartment.

One time, a girl sat next to her mother in his compartment. The girl was reading a book that just happened to be *Alice's Adventures in Wonderland.* Mr. Dodgson asked the girl if the book was any good.

"*Very* good," said the girl.

"Isn't it sad," said the girl's mother, "about poor Mr. Lewis Carroll. He's gone mad, you know."

"Indeed," said Mr. Dodgson. "I had never heard that."

Agnes Florence Price

Dorothy Kitchin

Xie Kitchin

"Oh, I assure you it is quite true," said the mother. "I have it on the best authority."

Before Mr. Dodgson stepped off the train, he asked for the girl's address so he could send her a little gift. A few days later, she received a copy of *Through the Looking-Glass.* Mr. Dodgson had written her name in the book, adding: "From the Author, in memory of a pleasant journey."

During his summer vacation, he usually went to the seaside resort of Eastbourne. There he met lots of children on the beach. In those days children had to be fully dressed when they played on the beach. He used to ask the parents if their children could at least take off their gloves. And he lent the girls safety pins to pin up their skirts. Then they could wade out into the water — at least a little way.

Several different theaters staged *Alice's Adventures in Wonderland* as a play. Mr. Dodgson would go to the rehearsals. He usually got to know the girl who was playing Alice. Isa Bowman was one of those child-friends. When she grew up, she wrote a book about how much fun she had had with Mr. Dodgson when she was a child.

Ellen Terry was another of those child actresses (and later so were her younger sisters). Mr. Dodgson continued his friendship with Ellen Terry even after she had grown up.

Beatrice Hatch

Irene MacDonald

Agnes Hughes

Polly and Florence Terry

Dymphna and Mary Ellis with a friend

Nov. 6, 1893.

My dear Edith,
I was very much pleased to get your nice little letter: and I hope you won't mind letting Maud have the Nursery Alice, now that you have got the real one. Some day I will send you the other book about Alice, called "Through the Looking-Glass" but you had better not have it just yet, for fear you

Looking-glass letter to Edith Hall

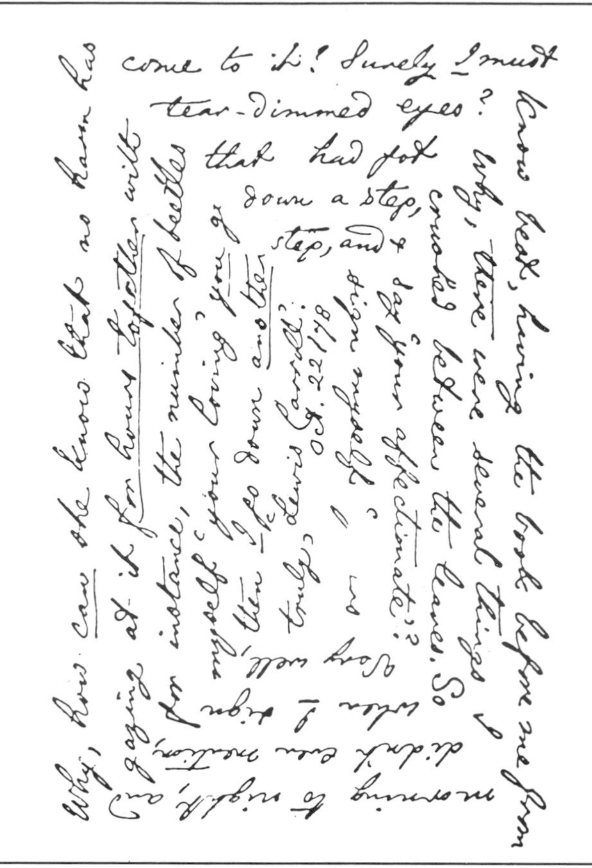

Why, how can she know that no harm has come to it? Surely I must know best, having the book before me from morning to night, and gazing at it for hours together with tear-dimmed eyes? Why, there were several things I didn't even notice, for instance, the number of beetles that had got crushed between the leaves. So when I sign myself 'your loving', you go down a step, and say 'your affectionate'? Very well, then I go down another step, and sign myself 'yours truly, Lewis Carroll.'
Oct. 22/78

Spiral letter to Agnes Hull

Mirror Letters, Rebus Letters, Cat Letters ...

• Mr. Dodgson loved to write letters. On January 1, 1861, he started numbering all the letters he sent and received. A couple of weeks before he died, he noted the last letter: 98,721!

Many of his pen pals were children. The letters he wrote to them were often imaginative. Sometimes he wrote backwards (with the last word on top) or spiraled (works inward and ends in the middle). Some letters were riddles, rebuses, or jokes.

In a letter to Agnes Hughes, daughter of the artist Arthur Hughes, he tells about *a very curious thing that happened to me at half-past four yesterday. Three visitors came knocking at my door, begging me to let them in. And when I opened the door, who do you think they were? You'll never guess. Why, they were three cats! Wasn't it curious? However, they all looked so cross and disagreeable that I took up the first thing I could lay my hand on (which happened to be the rolling-pin) and knocked them all down as flat as pancakes!*

Apparently Agnes had thought that was quite brutal, as she soon got another letter:

My Dear Agnes,

About the cats, you know. Of course I didn't leave them lying flat on the ground like dried flowers! No, I picked them up, and I was as kind as I could be to them. I lent them a portfolio for a bed — they wouldn't have been comfortable in a real bed, you know: they were too thin — but they were quite *happy between the sheets of blotting-paper — and each of them had a penwiper for a pillow.*

In the morning I gave them some rat-tail jelly and buttered mice for breakfast, and they were as discontented as they could be. They wanted some boiled pelican, but of course I knew it wouldn't be good for them.

Here's what he wrote to Beatrice Hatch, one of the Reverend Edwin Hatch's little daughters:

My Dear Birdie,

I met her just outside Tom Gate, walking very stiffly, and I think she was trying to find her way to my rooms. So I said,

The

My Ina,
Though don't give birthday presents, still
April . . . write a birthday .
June came 2 your 2
wish U many happy returns
of the day, the met
me, took me for a ,
hunted me and
till could hardly
However somehow got
into the , there
a met me, took me
for a , and pelted me

Rebus letter to Georgina Watson

Nov. 1. 1891.
C.L.D., Uncle loving
your! Instead grand
-son his to it give to
had you that so, years
80 or 70 for it forgot
you that was it pity
a what and: him of fond
so were you wonder don't
I and, gentleman old
nice very a was he. For
it made you that him
been have must it see
you so: grandfather my
was, then alive was that,
"Dodgson Uncle" only
the. Born was I before

Backwards letter to Nellie Bowman

"Why have you come here without Birdie?" So she said, "Birdie's gone! and Emily's gone! and Mabel isn't kind to me!" And two little waxy tears came running down her cheeks.

Why, how stupid of me! I've never told you who it was all the time! It was your new doll. I was very glad to see her, and I took her to my room, and gave her some vesta matches to eat, and a cup of nice melted wax to drink, for the poor little thing was very *hungry and thirsty after her long walk. So I said, "Come and sit down by the fire, and let's have a comfortable chat." "Oh no!* No*!" she said. "I'd* much *rather not. You know I do melt so* very *easily!" And she made me take her quite to the other side of the room, where it was* very *cold: and then she sat on my knee, and fanned herself with a penwiper because she said she was afraid the end of her nose was beginning to melt.*

"You've no idea *how careful we have to be, we dolls," she said.*

The doll (which, by the way, was named Alice) had been a present from Mr. Dodgson. Like those of many dolls in those days, its head and hands were made of wax, which was very sensitive to heat. It could say "Mama" and "Papa" if you squeezed its stomach. Emily and Mabel, who are named in the letter, were two of Beatrice's other dolls. Her sister Evelyn told this story in a book she wrote as an adult. The book also included many of Mr. Dodgson's letters to children that Evelyn had collected.

Here is another letter, this one about the weather, but not in the usual style.

My Dear Child,

It's been so frightfully hot here that I've been almost too weak to hold a pen, and even if I had been able, there was no ink — it had all evaporated into a cloud of black steam, and in that state it has been floating about the room, inking the walls and ceiling till they're hardly fit to be seen: to-day it is cooler, and a little has come back into the ink-bottle in the form of black snow — there will soon be enough for me to write and order those photographs your Mamma wants.

Your affectionate Friend,
Charles L. Dodgson.

The above letter was written to Mary MacDonald, Greville's sister and daughter of the author George MacDonald.

Mr. Dodgson's last picture of Alice, taken, according to his diary, on June 25, 1870

Edith, Alice, and Ina. Date unknown. May have been taken by Mr. Dodgson

Above and to the right: Sometimes Alice posed for Julia Margaret Cameron

How Alice's Life Continued…

● The Liddell girls were now grownup. Lorina married a rich man, and moved to Scotland. Harry married into money as well, and now Edith was to become engaged to Aubrey Harcourt, whose father owned Nuneham Park.

What about Alice? Here's how it was:

Queen Victoria's fourth son, Prince Leopold, was now a student at Christ Church. Alice's father was responsible for his education, and Dr. Acland for his health. The Prince was a good student, pleasant, and well educated. Unfortunately, he was also sickly; he had hemophilia (an inherited disease then common among European royalty). The tiniest little cut was life-threatening, because it could cause him to bleed to death.

The Prince visited the Liddells often. He and Alice fell in love, but the Queen had already decided that her sons would marry princesses. It was out of the question that the Prince would be allowed to marry Alice Liddell.

Just when Edith and Aubrey were about to announce their engagement, Edith became ill. At first they thought it was measles, but she got worse and developed terrible stomach pains. Dr. Acland couldn't do anything for her. On June 26, 1876, she died of peritonitis, and was buried at Christ Church.

Alice was no longer a happy girl: her favorite sister was dead, and she couldn't marry the man she was in love with.

After a few years it was decided that the Prince would marry a German princess. Their first child was christened Alice.

Before that, Alice had met another Christ Church student, Reginald ("Regi") Hargreaves. He was good-looking, but not much of a student. When he finally managed to pass his exams, he and Alice got engaged.

They had a magnificent society wedding in Westminster Abbey in London, no less. Rhoda and Violet were maids of honor. Alice was a beautiful bride. On her wedding dress she had pinned a pearl horseshoe brooch that the Prince had given her. The list of Alice's wedding presents includes the names of 137 people, but no Mr. Dodgson.

So Alice became Mrs. Reginald Hargreaves and moved to an enormous house that Regi had inherited in Lyndhurst (some eighty miles south of Oxford, near Southampton).

There Alice was in charge of a butler, a housekeeper, a chief cook, two kitchen maids, a scullery maid (who washed the dishes), a laundry maid, a head housemaid and her two assistants, two footmen, two chambermaids, and a doorman.

Alice was interested in painting, singing, reading, and intellectual conversation. Regi, however, had other

Alice in New York, 1932. Photo by W. Colbourn Brown

interests: cricket, golf, horses, hunting, and business. It couldn't have been all that easy for Alice to give up the cultivated Oxford life.

Alice and Regi had three sons: Alan, Rex, and Caryl (pronounced "Carroll"). They were young men in 1914, when World War I broke out, and all three of them went off to war. In 1915 Alan was killed, and in 1916 Rex. That left Alice with only one son.

Alice's husband died when she was seventy-three years old. After his death, Alice decided to sell some of her belongings, among them Mr. Dodgson's handwritten book. (Nobody can explain why.) She gave it to Sotheby's in London to be auctioned off. The book was sold to an American antique-book dealer named Rosenbach for £15,400. That was the most money ever paid for a book in England.

When she was eighty years old, Alice was invited to the United States to celebrate the hundredth anniversary of Lewis Carroll's birth. Her son Caryl and her sister Rhoda went over with her on the big Atlantic steamer *Berengaria*.

In New York, there was great excitement about her visit, and photographers followed her everywhere. She had to give speeches and open exhibitions. She even received an honorary degree from Columbia University. Oh, how exhausted Alice was by it all!

Dr. Rosenbach had already sold the book to someone else — a millionaire named Eldridge Johnson — for $150,000. Alice was invited to Dr. Rosenbach's home. Mr. Johnson came, too. He arrived with a water- and fireproof metal box. In it was Alice's book; she had the honor of being able to look at it. That must have seemed very odd to her . . .

Alice survived her trip to America, even though she once said she almost wished she hadn't been "the real Alice."

Alice died two years later, on November 15, 1934. She was buried at Lyndhurst.

P.S. Neither Rhoda nor Violet ever married. They were simply not interested in taking on the role of wife, as Ina and Alice had done, but wanted to be free to devote themselves to the feminist movement and to art (wood sculpture). Edith's fiancé never married, either.

Miss Prickett, however, did get married. When the Liddells didn't need her services any longer, she was thirty-eight years old. It was then she met a wine merchant who was a widower and who owned the Mitre Hotel in Oxford. So she became Mrs. Charles Foster. After her husband's death, she took over as sole owner of the hotel, which still stands on the High today (now just a restaurant).

... and How M

● Mr. Dodgson remained single, staying on at Christ Church all his life. But he moved to more elegant quarters that had, among other things, two little tower rooms where children often played. Up on the roof was a photographic studio he had built.

During vacations he lived in the town of Guildford. In 1868, after his father's death, he rented a house there for his six unmarried sisters. (Only three of the eleven Dodgson brothers and sisters ever married, and that wasn't until after their father's death.)

Mr. Dodgson wrote some other children's books (for example, *Sylvie and Bruno*), but they were not a success. On the other hand, *The Hunting of the Snark* is a remarkable story written in verse. He started by writing the last line first (*For the snark was a boojum, you see*); then he had to write the rest of the poem to go with the ending. But what was a snark?

"I have no idea," Mr. Dodgson might have answered, if you had asked him.

Under his real name, Mr. Dodgson wrote a number of books on mathematics. Bertrand Russell (mathematician,

Above: *A self-portrait, taken by Mr. Dodgson in 1895, when he was sixty-three*

Right: *Mr. Dodgson's sitting room. He moved here in October 1868. The tiles around the fireplace were designed by William De Morgan, showing different animals (such as a dodo). Mr. Dodgson ordered them and would tell stories about them for his young guests.*

Probably Bob the Bat is in the upper left desk drawer (behind the sofa)

Far right: Through the Looking-Glass, *performed by children from the Myra Lodge School (Hampstead, London, 1908 or 1910)*

Dodgson Lived

philosopher, and Nobel Prize winner) considered several of Mr. Dodgson's theories to be revolutionary.

Mr. Dodgson was very interested in the latest inventions. When he saw the first phonograph (forerunner of the record player), he wished that he had been born fifty years later. He could see then that something fantastic would come of it. Imagine what fun he could have had with a computer! The inventions he thought up (something like double-sided cellophane tape and improvements on the bicycle) were not produced during his lifetime.

Think how he would have enjoyed our fast, lightweight cameras. He is still considered one of England's best photographers of children. Some people have suggested he might have been a little strange, since he sometimes took pictures of children naked. But we have to remember that, in Victorian times, it was fashionable to have children photographed in this manner. Often the picture was then given to an artist, who would color it and add a romantic painting in the background. Sometimes he would even paint wings on the children to make them look like little fairies. Just think — children could be naked in pictures, but they had to wear gloves on the beach!

The children had to think it was fun to take off their clothes, said Mr. Dodgson; otherwise, he would not consider taking such a photograph. Besides, their mother or a chaperone always came with them to the studio, so it must have all been very proper.

Mr. Dodgson became more and more of a loner and was considered, in Oxford, to be quite eccentric. He hated all the attention he got as a world-famous author.

Alice hadn't seen him for many years when she got this letter one day:

Christ Church, Oxford, March 1, 1885

My Dear Mrs. Hargreaves,

I fancy this will come to you almost like a voice from the dead, after so many years of silence — and yet those years have made no difference, that I can perceive, in my *clearness of memory of the days when we* did *correspond. - - - My mental picture is as vivid as ever, of one who was, through so many years, my ideal child-friend. I have had scores of child-friends since your time: but they have been quite a different thing.*

Now, Mr. Dodgson wasn't just writing to tell her that. He also wanted to ask if Alice had anything against his publishing the handwritten book in facsimile (printed copy of the original).

Alice saved that letter as long as she lived; now she was the only one who decided which letters would be destroyed or saved.

In 1897 Mr. Dodgson spent Christmas with his sisters, as usual. But he was in bed with a bad cold. It moved down into his bronchial tubes and lungs, and since this was long before the discovery of penicillin, he became seriously ill.

On the afternoon of January 14, 1898, Mr. Dodgson died, just two weeks before his sixty-sixth birthday. He was buried in Guildford. Alice didn't attend his funeral. She did send flowers, however, which, along with many others, covered his coffin.

Even though Mr. Dodgson and his ideal child-friend have been dead such a long time, the story that he wrote for her lives on. Many new generations of children will come to read it, or maybe remember how they performed *Alice's Adventures in Wonderland* or *Through the Looking-Glass* when they were children in school.

"And I was Alice . . ." someone will proudly explain, just like the girl in the middle of the picture below, Ruth Dingley, who, when this was written, * was ninety-six years old and a great-grandmother. She has given her own cherished copy of *Alice* to her granddaughter Kate, who soon will be reading it for her little Maja . . .

* Stockholm, April 1993

This and That...

Alice, Ina, Harry, and Edith, 1859.

The Handwritten Manuscript

which Mr. Dodgson gave Alice is now in the British Library in London. Go to the British Museum on Great Russell Street, use the main entrance and then turn right and go through the British Library's bookstore. The next room is the manuscript hall. There in a glass case you can see *Alice's Adventures Under Ground.*

Mr. Dodgson's family

His father: Charles Dodgson, 1800–1868

His mother: Frances Jane (born Lutwidge), 1803–1851

Their children:
Frances Jane (Fanny), 1828–1903
Elizabeth Lucy, 1830–1916
Charles Lutwidge, 1832–1898
Caroline Hume, 1833–1904
Mary Charlotte, 1835–1911, married
Skeffington Hume, 1836–1919, married
Wilfred Longley, 1838–1914, married to Alice Jane Donkin (see page 51)
Louisa Fletcher, 1840–1930
Margaret Anne Ashley, 1841–1915
Henrietta Harington, 1843–1922
Edwin Heron, 1846–1918

Queen Victoria's family

The Queen: 1819–1901 (reigned 1837–1901)

The Prince Consort: Albert of Saxe-Coburg-Gotha, 1819–1861

Their children:
Victoria, Edward, Alice, Alfred, Helena, Louise, Arthur, Leopold, Beatrice

Alice Liddell's family

Alice's father: Henry George Liddell, 1811–1898

Alice's mother: Lorina Hannah (born Reeve), 1826–1910

Their children:
Edward Henry (Harry), 1847–1911
Lorina Charlotte, 1849–1930
James Arthur Charles, 1850–1853
Alice Pleasance, 1852–1934
Edith Mary, 1854–1876
Rhoda Caroline Anne, 1859–1949
Albert Edward Arthur, 1863–1863
Violet Constance, 1864–1927
Frederick Francis (Eric), 1865–1950
Lionel Charles, 1868–1942

... and When and What

Books Published under the Name Lewis Carroll

(some of them)

1865 Alice's Adventures in Wonderland
1871 Through the Looking-Glass
1876 The Hunting of the Snark
1886 Alice's Adventures Underground (facsimile)
1889 The Nursery Alice (shortened version)
1889 Sylvie and Bruno
1890 Eight or Nine Wise Words about Letter Writing
1893 Sylvie and Bruno Concluded

Books and Articles Published under the Name C. L. Dodgson

(some of them)

1858 The Fifth Book of Euclid Treated Algebraically
1860 Rules for Court Circular
Syllabus of Plane Algebraical Geometry
Notes on the first two books of Euclid
1863 Croquet Castles
Enunciations of Euclid, Books I and II
1866 Condensation of Determinants
1874 Suggestions as to the Best Method of Taking Votes
1879 Euclid and His Modern Rivals
Doublets — A word puzzle
1884 Principals of Parliamentary Representation
1885 A Tangled Tale (reprinted from *The Monthly Packet*)
1886 The Game of Logic
Curiosa Mathematica, Part I — a new theory of parallels
1893 Curiosa Mathematica, Part II — Pillow Problems
1896 Symbolic Logic

Societies for Alice and Carroll Friends

The Lewis Carroll Society

Chairman: Anne Clark Amor
Treasurer: Roger Allen, 146 Headstone Lane, Harrow, HA2 6JT, England (U.K.)
Meetings are once a month. It publishes a magazine, *Jabberwocky* (editor, Selwyn Goodacre), and a newsletter, *Bandersnatch* (editor, Alfreda Blanchard). There are members all over the world. Annual dues are about £10. (Write to the treasurer for the exact amount.)

Lewis Carroll Society of North America

Address: 617 Rockford Road, Silver Spring, MD 20902, U.S.A.
Newsletter: *Knight Letter.*

Lewis Carroll Birthplace Trust

An organization working to establish a Carroll museum in Daresbury, Cheshire, England, Lewis Carroll's birthplace.

The Dodo Club

Membership limited to children, adults can be "associates." Annual dues (in Europe) are £5 (£10 for associates). Outside of Europe, dues are £12. The organizer is Alan Holland, 89 Ffordd Pentre, Mold, Clwyd, CH7 1UY, Wales (U.K.).
Mr. Holland is also the editor of *Dodo Club News,* full or riddles, verses, children's letters, and tips. Among other things, you can learn that *"Alice's Adventures in Wonderland* by Lewis Carroll" contains exactly 42 letters!

Alice Club

Open only to "friends of Alice" who are students at Oxford.

What Was Under the Nursery Floor?

● Remember Mr. Dodgson's secret treasures, which he hid under the nursery floor at Croft rectory when he was a boy? (See page 45.)

When the house was renovated in the 1950s, the following things were found under the floor:

One well-used left shoe
One white glove (the one the rabbit is missing in *Alice's Adventures in Wonderland*?)
One doll-size teapot lid
One thimble (Alice had one in her pocket in the story)
Bits of crab shell (also in the story)
The letter S from an alphabet game

Solutions to:

More cakes in a row (page 63)

1.

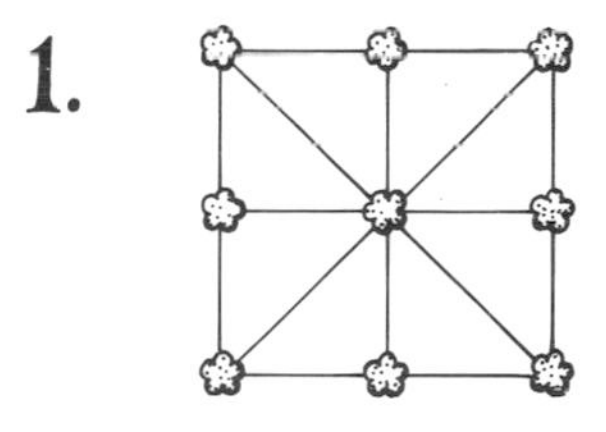

2.

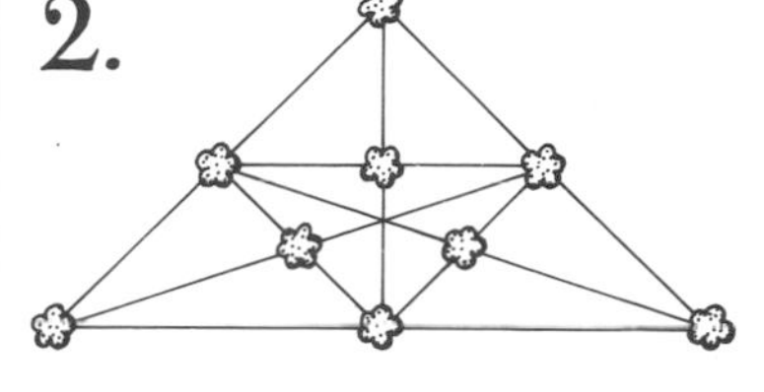

Oxford Is the Same as Ever

• If you ignore the traffic and the modern clothes, it feels almost as if you could meet Mr. Dodgson and the Liddell girls on any street corner. But the most likely place would probably be in Christ Church.

① Mr. Dodgson's window is on the second floor, between the towers far left of Tom Tower (seen from St. Aldate's Street). The Oxford colleges are open to visitors at varying times.

② You'll be admitted to Christ Church by the friendly "bulldogs" (guards wearing bowler hats).

③ From Tom Quad, you'll easily find Alice's front door. The Deanery is next door, and Mr. Dodgson lived at staircase number 7, across Tom Quad. Unfortunately, you can't go in. Alice's house is now the dean's private quarters. Mr. Dodgson's room is now the Graduate Common Room.

The Hall, the impressive dining room where Mr. Dodgson ate his meals, on the other hand, is open certain hours. Pictures of Mr. Dodgson, Dean Liddell, and many other people hang there. One window is decorated with *Alice* designs. The brass figures by the fireplace might have given Mr. Dodgson the idea for Alice's incredibly long neck in the story.

④ Christ Church Cathedral is open during the daytime except when in use. One of the windows (by Burne-Jones) shows St. Frideswide (center). Edith Liddell was the model.

Near the cathedral is the Chapter House, with its fine souvenir shop. Among other things you can find there are two excellent booklets (about £2 each). *Alice's Adventures in Oxford* by Mavis Batey (Pitkin Pictorials, Andover, 1989); *Oxford's Gargoyles and Grotesques* by John Blackwood and David Collett (Charon Press, Oxford, 1986).

⑤ Visit Christ Church Picture Gallery, a fine little art museum. Perhaps Alice saw *The Wounded Centaur,* painted by Filippino Lippi in the fifteenth century. (And perhaps she also looked inside the cave.) In Alice's time, the Picture Gallery was in New Library.

Alice's Shop is also a souvenir shop, at 83 St. Aldate's Street. Alice came here with Phoebe to buy sugar candy. The tourist information center is on

①

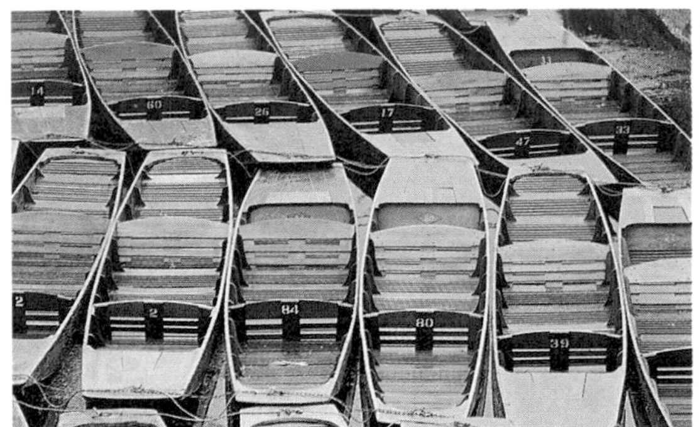

⑦

⑧

②

⑨

Don't Forget Your Binoculars!

St. Aldate's, but nearer Queen Street.
⑥ The Botanic Garden has built a new water-lily building since Alice's day; the monkeys are gone, but the ginkgo tree is still there. Buy a guide booklet if you want a map showing all the trees in the Garden, and the years they were planted.
⑦ Next to Magdalen Bridge, you can rent a punt (a boat you move along by pushing a pole against the bottom of the shallow, winding river Cherwell).
⑧ and ⑨ Magdalen College is near the Botanic Garden. Don't miss the monsters (see page 68) in the courtyard and the deer park. Take a peek into the porter's room by the entrance; you'll see a collection of teddy bears. Students traditionally leave their mascots there after graduation.
⑩ Mr. Dodgson's camera is in the History of Science Museum on Broad Street.
⑪ Here is another dodo painting. Next to the museum is the Sheldonian Theatre, guarded by "emperor heads," now restored (see page 74). Nice view from the cupola. Almost opposite is Blackwell's bookstore, established in 1879. You can get another good view of Oxford from the top of Carfax Tower at Queen Street.
⑫ Not far from here is the University Museum on Parks Road, where you can see the dodo remains and the dodo painting (plus a lot of other things). Don't forget to look at the gargoyle windows.
⑬ You can still rent a rowboat at Salters' by Folly Bridge (south of Christ Church), but they aren't as beautiful as they were in Alice's day.
⑭ If you're strong enough, you can row to Binsey, or you can walk along the paths by the river with its beautiful countryside and nice cows. (Godstow is a bit farther on.) The treacle well (page 59) is in the graveyard, next to the church. Several of the gravestones say Prickett on them, but Miss Prickett herself isn't buried here.
⑮ The easiest way to Nuneham Park is by bus from Oxford Coach Station (bus station). One picnic shelter is still there. Ask the landowner first if you are thinking about going down to the river.

⑩

⑪

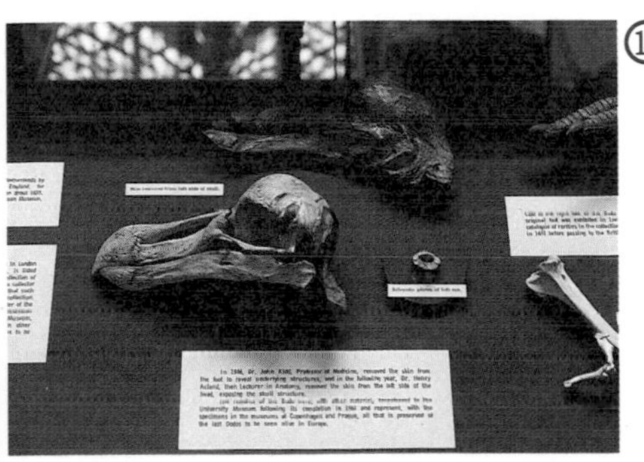
⑫

⑤

⑥

⑬

⑭

⑮

Bibliography

• These are some of the books we used as sources for our book. Unfortunately, many of them are old and difficult to get. One place to look is antiquarian bookstores, especially in England. Otherwise, try the library.

Alice's Adventures in Wonderland, Through the Looking-Glass, and *The Hunting of the Snark* are available in several different editions at most bookstores.

Mr. Dodgson's Diaries and Letters

- Cohen, Morton N., ed. *The Letters of Lewis Carroll,* Vols. 1 and 2. London: Macmillan, 1979; New York: Oxford University Press, 1979.
- Cohen, Morton N., ed. *The Selected Letters of Lewis Carroll.* London: Macmillan; New York: Pantheon, 1982.
- Green, Roger Lancelyn, ed. *The Diaries of Lewis Carroll,* Vols. 1 and 2. London: Cassell & Co., 1953.
- Hatch, Evelyn. *A Selection from the Letters of Lewis Carroll to His Child-Friends.* London: Macmillan, 1933.
- Hinde, Thomas, ed. *Looking-Glass Letters.* London: Collins & Brown, 1991; New York: Rizzoli, 1992.
- Wakeling, Edward, ed. *The Complete Diaries of Lewis Carroll.* Oxford: The Lewis Carroll Birthplace Trust, 1993.

Mr. Dodgson's Photography

- Almansi, Guido, ed. *Lewis Carroll. Photos and Letters to His Child Friends.* Parma: Franco Maria Ricci, 1975.
- Gattegno, Jean. *Album Lewis Carroll.* Paris: Gallimard (Bibliothèque de la Pléiade), 1990.
- Gernsheim, Helmut. *Lewis Carroll: Photographer.* New York: Dover, 1969.

Mr. Dodgson's Magazines, Verses, and Other Works with Commentaries

- Carroll, Lewis. *The Rectory Umbrella and Mischmasch.* New York: Dover, 1971.
- Collingwood, Stuart Dodgson. *The Life and Letters of Lewis Carroll.* London: Thomas Nelson & Sons, 1899; New York: Reprint Service, 1992.

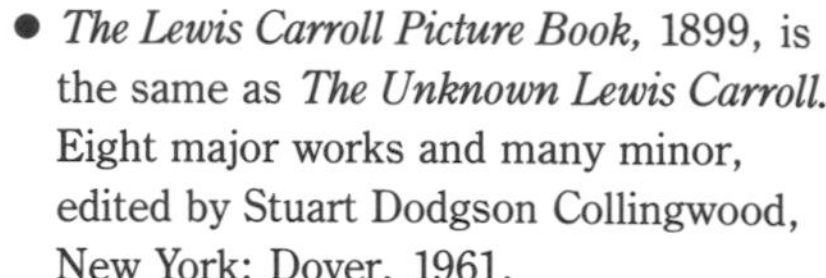

- *The Lewis Carroll Picture Book,* 1899, is the same as *The Unknown Lewis Carroll.* Eight major works and many minor, edited by Stuart Dodgson Collingwood, New York: Dover, 1961.
- *The Humorous Verses of Lewis Carroll.* New York: Dover, 1960 (First published 1933).
- Gardner, Martin. *The Annotated Alice.* New York: NAL/Dutton, 1974.
- Gardner, Martin. *The Wasp in a Wig by Lewis Carroll.* London: Macmillan, 1977.
- Gardner, Martin. *More Annotated Alice.* New York: Random House, 1990.
- Gardner, Martin. *The Annotated Snark.* New York: Simon & Schuster, 1962; London: Penguin, 1967.

Mr. Dodgson's Puzzles and Games

- Fisher, John. *The Magic of Lewis Carroll.* London: Thomas Nelson and Sons, 1973.
- Gardner, Martin. *The Snark Puzzle Book.* New York: Simon & Schuster, 1973; New York: Prometheus, 1990.
- Wakeling, Edward. *Lewis Carroll's Games and Puzzles.* New York: Dover, 1992.

Biographies and Recollections

- Batey, Mavis. *The Adventures of Alice.* London: Macmillan, 1991.
- Bowman, Isa. *The Story of Lewis Carroll.* London: J. M. Dent, 1899.
- Clark, Anne. *Lewis Carroll: A Biography.* London: J. M. Dent & Sons, 1979.
- Clark, Anne. *The Real Alice.* London: Michael Joseph, 1981.
- Cohen, Morton N. *Lewis Carroll: Interviews and Recollections.* London: Macmillan, 1989; Iowa: University of Iowa Press, 1989.
- Gattegno, Jean. *Lewis Carroll, une vie: D'Alice à Zénon d'Elée.* Paris: Editions du Seuil, 1974. In English under the title *Fragments of a Looking-Glass.* New York: Thomas Y. Crowell, 1976.

- Gordon, Colin. *Beyond the Looking-Glass.* New York: Harcourt Brace Jovanovitch, 1982.
- Green, Roger Lancelyn. *The Story of Lewis Carroll.* London: Methuen, 1949 (written for children from ten and up).
- Green, Roger Lancelyn. *Lewis Carroll.* London: Bodley Head, 1960.
- Hargreaves, Caryl. *Alice's Recollections from Carrollian Days.* Cornhill Magazine, 1932.
- Hudson, Derek. *Lewis Carroll: An Illustrated Biography.* London: Constable, 1954 and 1982; New York: Greenwood, 1972.
- Lennon, Florence Becker. *Lewis Carroll.* London: Cassell & Co., 1947.

Essays on Lewis Carroll's Works

- Giuliano, Edward, ed. *Lewis Carroll: A Celebration.* Essays on the Occasion of the 150th Anniversary of the Birth of Charles Lutwidge Dodgson. New York: Clarkson N. Potter, 1982.
- Phillips, Robert, ed. *Aspects of Alice.* London: Penguin, 1971; New York: Vanguard, 1971.

Miscellaneous

- Batey, Mavis. *Oxford Gardens.* Amersham: Avebury Publishing Company, 1982; Atlanta: Scolar Press, 1986.
- Newman, Cathy and Sam Abell. *The Wonderland of Lewis Carroll.* Washington: National Geographic, 1991.

List of Illustrations and Copyrights

Abbreviations

Christ Church = The Governing Body of Christ Church, Oxford University
Evelyn Hatch = Evelyn Hatch: *A Selection from the Letters of Lewis Carroll to his Child-Friends* (see Bibliography)
Gernsheim Collection = Gernsheim Collection, Harry Ransom Humanities Research Center, The University of Texas at Austin
Life and Letters = Stuart Dodgson Collingwood: *The Life and Letters of Lewis Carroll* (see Bibliography)
Macmillan = Macmillan Publishers, London

5, 18, 19 Christ Church
9 Macmillan
20 Self portrait: Life and Letters
21, 24 Christ Church
26 University Museum, Oxford
32 Graham Ovenden
33, 34 Christ Church
36–37 Gernsheim Collection, 1842 Mines Report, *London Labour and the London Poor,* 1861
51 Collingwood: L. C. Picture Book (see Bibliography)
52, 55, 61 Christ Church
64–65 Life and Letters
72 Mansell Collection, London
73 Wilfred's gryphon: Christ Church; MacDonald children: Christie's Images
76–77 Macmillan
78 Macmillan, British Library, William Heinemann, London, 1907, © Robert Högfeldt/BUS, Stockholm, 1993.
79 Macmillan; Tove Jansson: Bonniers, Stockholm, 1966; Franz Haacken: Georg Bitter Verlag, Recklinghausen, 1968; Nicole Claveloux: Editions Grasset & Fasquelle, Paris, 1974; © Salvador Dali: Demart Pro Arte/BUS, Stockholm, 1993.
80–81 Graham Ovenden, (pictures 1, 2, 3, and 8) Gernsheim Collection
82–83 Evelyn Hatch
84–85 Christ Church
86 Gernsheim Collection, Christ Church (the room)
87 Ruth Dingley/Kate Meurling
88–89 Christ Church
91 Christ Church Picture Gallery (5)
92–93 Nisse Peterson, Christ Church
Cover and jacket flap: Macmillan, Christ Church, Nisse Peterson

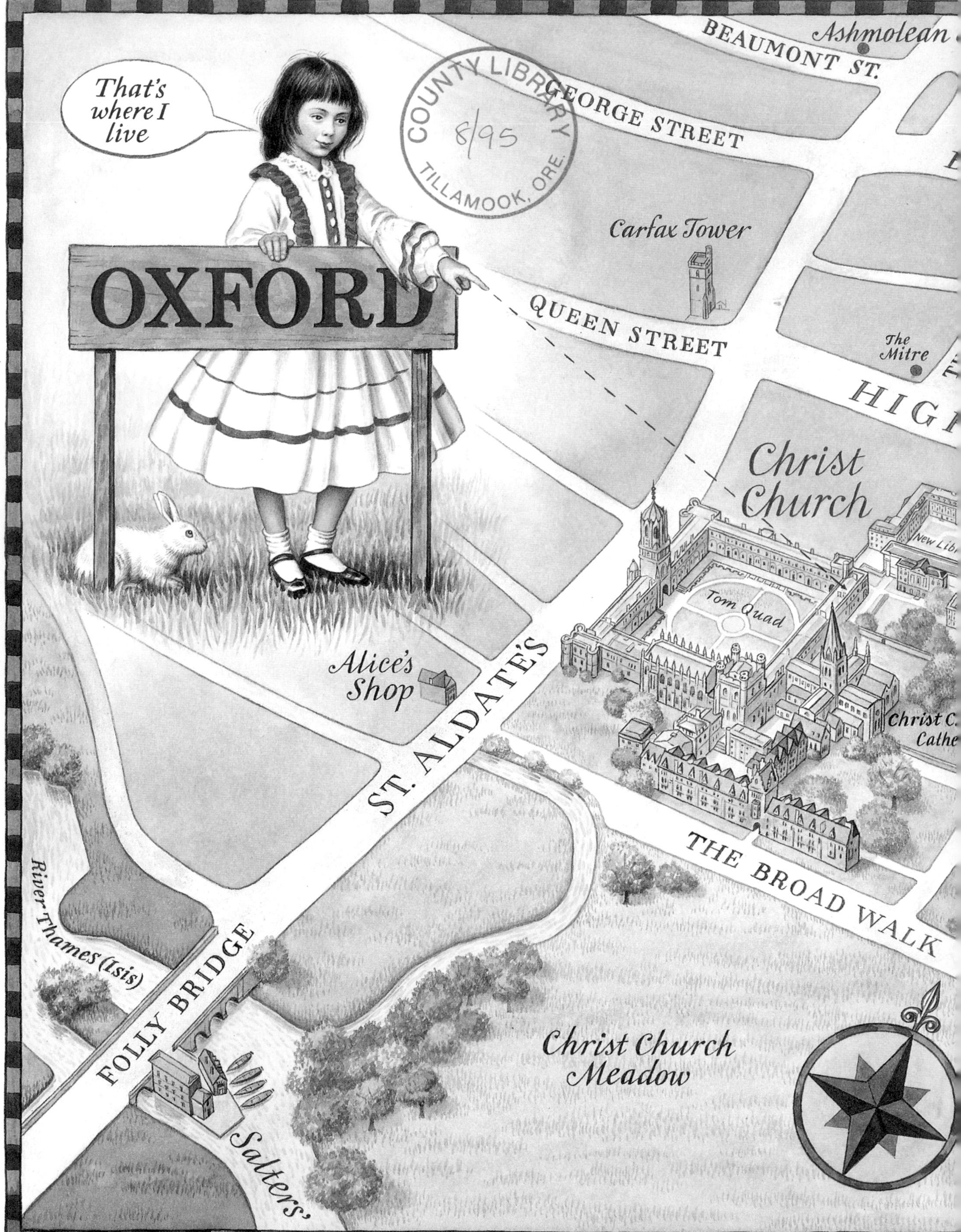
That's where I live
OXFORD
Ashmolean
BEAUMONT ST.
GEORGE STREET
Carfax Tower
QUEEN STREET
The Mitre
Christ Church
Tom Quad
Alice's Shop
ST. ALDATE'S
THE BROAD WALK
River Thames (Isis)
FOLLY BRIDGE
Salters'
Christ Church Meadow